THE PUSH
FOR **SOCIAL**
CHANGE

The Civil Rights Movement

Craig E. Blohm

ReferencePoint
Press®

San Diego, CA

About the Author

Craig E. Blohm has written numerous books and magazine articles for young readers. He and his wife, Desiree, reside in Tinley Park, Illinois.

© 2019 ReferencePoint Press, Inc.
Printed in the United States

For more information, contact:
ReferencePoint Press, Inc.
PO Box 27779
San Diego, CA 92198
www.ReferencePointPress.com

LIBRARY OF CONGRESS CATALOGING-IN-PUBLICATION DATA

Names: Blohm, Craig E., 1948– author.
Title: The Civil Rights Movement/by Craig E. Blohm.
Description: San Diego, CA: ReferencePoint Press, Inc., 2019. | Series: The Push for Social Change | Includes bibliographical references and index. | Audience: Grades 9–12.
Identifiers: LCCN 2018017166 (print) | LCCN 2018018167 (ebook) | ISBN 9781682824207 (eBook) | ISBN 9781682824191 (hardback)
Subjects: LCSH: African Americans—Civil rights—History—Juvenile literature. | Civil rights movements—United States—History—20th century—Juvenile literature. | United States—Race relations—Juvenile literature.
Classification: LCC E185.61 (ebook) | LCC E185.61 .B667 2019 (print) | DDC 323.1196/073—dc23
LC record available at https://lccn.loc.gov/2018017166

CONTENTS

IMPORTANT EVENTS IN THE CIVIL RIGHTS MOVEMENT

1865
The Thirteenth Amendment to the Constitution abolishes slavery.

1920
The Nineteenth Amendment gives women the right to vote.

1870
The Fifteenth Amendment bans discrimination in voting.

1948
President Harry S. Truman desegregates the armed forces.

1860　1885　1910　1935　1960

1868
The Fourteenth Amendment affirms citizenship rights and equal protection under the law.

1954
Brown v. Board of Education declares school segregation unconstitutional.

1955
Rosa Parks refuses to give up her seat on a Montgomery, Alabama, bus.

1957
The Little Rock Nine integrate Central High School in Little Rock, Arkansas.

1960
Four college students stage a sit-in at a Woolworth's lunch counter in Greensboro, North Carolina.

4

1961
Freedom Riders are attacked in Montgomery, Alabama.

1963
Two hundred thousand people join the March on Washington for Jobs and Freedom.

1964
President Lyndon B. Johnson signs the Civil Rights Act of 1964.

2008
Barack Obama is elected the first African American president of the United States.

1965   1970 / 2000   2005   2015

1968
Dr. Martin Luther King Jr. is assassinated in Memphis, Tennessee.

2013
The Black Lives Matter movement is founded by three women activists.

2018
For the second year in a row, hundreds of thousands of women march nationwide to protest government policies on a variety of issues; marchers focused on civil rights, women's rights, and human rights.

1972
The Equal Rights Amendment passes Congress, but is never ratified by the states.

1965
Violence erupts on the march from Selma to Montgomery, Alabama.

1962
James Meredith becomes the first black student to enroll at the University of Mississippi.

Equal Rights for All

On Sunday, July 16, 1854, Elizabeth Jennings hurried to the streetcar stop, worried that she would be late for church. The choir at the First Colored American Congregational Church on Sixth Street in New York City was waiting for the twenty-four-year-old African American schoolteacher to arrive. Jennings was the church organist, and rehearsal could not begin without her. But on that day, Jennings never arrived.

When a horse-drawn streetcar pulled up, Jennings got on. Immediately the driver told her to get off, because only whites were allowed in the vehicle. Jennings refused. "I told him I was a respectable person," she later said, recalling that she scolded the driver for "insulting decent persons while on their way to church."[1] Ultimately, a policeman forcibly removed Jennings from the streetcar. Bruised and aching, with her dress soiled and torn, Jennings returned home.

> "All men are created equal, [and] they are endowed by their Creator with certain unalienable rights."[2]
>
> —The Declaration of Independence

Just over one hundred years later, another African American woman stepped onto a segregated bus in Montgomery, Alabama. By refusing to give up her seat to a white passenger, Rosa Parks became a symbol of the modern struggle for civil rights. In the years between the two women's courageous actions, African Americans in the United States suffered from lack of educational and employment opportunities and exclusion from the basic rights afforded every American citizen. Some who stood up against the oppression—and many who did not—were punished, beaten, or even murdered because of their skin color. The Declaration of Independence proclaims that "all men are created equal, [and] they are endowed by their Creator with certain unalienable rights."[2]

It would take the civil rights movement, and the sacrifices of people too numerous to mention, to even begin to make that proclamation a reality.

A Long March to Freedom

The Civil War ended in 1865, eleven years after Elizabeth Jennings attempted to ride on a segregated New York streetcar. The war kept the nation together and dealt a death blow to slavery in the South. But gaining their freedom did not mean that African Americans were instantly given all their rights enumerated in the Declaration. Immediately after the Civil War ended, Southern states passed laws called Black Codes that restricted the freedom of former slaves and kept them working for minimal wages. These laws were the forerunners of Jim Crow laws that made segregation in schools, transportation, theaters, and other public areas legal. Outside of the law, white-supremacy groups such as the Ku

A painting depicts a battle scene from the Civil War, which ended in 1865. The war kept the nation together and dealt a death blow to slavery in the South.

Klux Klan (KKK) conducted a reign of terror throughout the South by kidnapping, beating, and lynching (putting a person to death, usually by hanging, without legal authorization) innocent blacks.

African Americans lived with these harsh realities for generations. The KKK suffered a decline in the late nineteenth century, but it experienced revivals in 1915 and after World War II. Jim Crow laws remained on the books until the middle of the twentieth century. It was then that brave people, both black and white, finally began to stand up in unison against injustice.

Heroes of the Civil Rights Movement

Although the story of Elizabeth Jennings is little known today, she was nevertheless an early hero in the struggle for civil rights. In the twentieth century many people took a stand for civil rights, often at the cost of their own lives. Rosa Parks refused to give up her seat on a bus in 1955. Two years later, nine African American students braved taunts and insults as they became the first minority students to enter Central High School in Little Rock, Arkansas. In 1960, four African American college students sat down at a segregated lunch counter in North Carolina. Although they were refused service, they remained until closing, returning to sit again the next day. It was an early example of the sit-in, a protest method that was used extensively during the Civil Rights Movement and later by students protesting the Vietnam War.

A group called the Freedom Riders rode buses through the South in 1961 to protest segregation in bus terminals and other transportation facilities. The riders, both black and white, met with violent protests that resulted in numerous injuries and a bus being burned. These seemingly small incidents paved the way for a movement by inspiring others to act.

Activists and Presidents

The most important event of the Civil Rights Movement was the March on Washington for Jobs and Freedom held on August 28,

1963. Spearheaded by civil rights leader Dr. Martin Luther King Jr., the march brought some 250,000 people to Washington, DC, to demonstrate for jobs and freedom. In what became a defining moment of the movement, Dr. King gave his stirring "I Have a Dream" speech, speaking before the crowd and a nationwide radio and television audience. King was not alone in fighting for civil rights. Activist Ralph Abernathy collaborated with King in organizing a bus boycott in Montgomery, Alabama. Ella Baker helped found the Student Nonviolent Coordinating Committee, which played a major role in civil rights protests of the 1960s.

When John F. Kennedy was elected president in 1960, Jim Crow laws were still widespread in the southern United States. During his campaign, Kennedy expressed his support for civil rights, and 70 percent of African American voters cast their ballots for Kennedy. They had high hopes that the young and charismatic president would advance the cause of civil rights, but international tensions kept Kennedy from concentrating on a domestic agenda. Then on November 22, 1963, Kennedy was assassinated in Dallas, Texas. It fell to his vice-president and successor, Lyndon B. Johnson, to take on the fight for civil rights. Johnson, a southerner, was up to the challenge, signing into law the Civil Rights Act of 1964 and the Voting Rights Act of 1965.

Since its founding, the United States has championed the ideal of equality for all its citizens. But ideals do not become reality by simply wishing them to be so; it is hard and often unsung work by dedicated people that brings an ideal to fruition. Through the dedication of the Civil Rights Movement, equality for all Americans was finally made the law of the land. Today, the legacy of that movement continues to fight discrimination and ensure that the nation remains true to its founding principles.

CHAPTER ONE

From Slavery to Jim Crow

On June 18, 1865, General Gordon Granger of the United States Army entered Galveston, Texas, as the new military governor of the former Confederate state. The Civil War had formally ended on April 9, when Confederate general Robert E. Lee surrendered to Union general Ulysses S. Grant at the village of Appomattox Court House in Virginia. With the chaos of battle and the era's slow communications, it took time for news of the end of the war to spread to all the former rebellious states. On Monday, June 19, Granger issued several orders establishing his authority as administrator of Texas. Of the five proclamations he signed, General Order No. 3 would be the most remembered. It read, in part: "The people of Texas are informed that, in accordance with a proclamation from the Executive of the United States, all slaves are free. This involves an absolute equality of personal rights and rights of property between former masters and slaves."[3] The Executive referred to in General Order No. 3 was President Abraham Lincoln, who had been assassinated five days after Lee's surrender. For the approximately 250,000 slaves laboring in the fields of Texas, freedom was finally at hand. To this day, many African Americans celebrate June 19 as *Juneteenth*, marking their own independence day.

Slavery in the South had been abolished in writing when Lincoln's Emancipation Proclamation, declaring that all slaves in the Confederate states were henceforth free, took effect on January 1, 1863. But with no way to enforce the proclamation during the war, it was, at best, a hollow victory for the slaves, most of whom were unaware of their new status. In addition, Lincoln feared that the Emancipation Proclamation, which was issued under his war powers authority, might be reversed after the war ended. To over-

President Lincoln (third from left) reviews a draft of the Emancipation Proclamation with his cabinet in 1862. The document abolished slavery in the nation.

come the inherent weakness of the Emancipation Proclamation, Lincoln knew that permanently ending slavery would require an amendment to the US Constitution.

Abolishing Slavery

As the Civil War entered its final years, legislators began to consider ways to implement a plan of Reconstruction to determine how the former Confederate states would be readmitted to the Union. During this period, which lasted from 1865 to 1877, three amendments to the Constitution addressed the rights and citizenship status of the South's former slaves, who were known after the war as freedmen.

In late 1863 and early 1864, several proposals for a Thirteenth Amendment abolishing slavery were introduced in Congress. While Republicans supported the proposals, Democrats, who feared that the proposed amendment would weaken the power of the individual states, remained opposed. In April 1864, a vote in the House of Representatives failed to adopt the amendment by a margin of thirteen votes. President Lincoln stepped up his commitment to abolishing slavery by making the amendment a part of his 1864 reelection platform. On January 31, 1865, Congress approved the Thirteenth Amendment and sent it to the states to be ratified. It was less than three months before Lee surrendered and an assassin's bullet cut short the life and postwar plans of Lincoln.

The Thirteenth Amendment was a landmark in the history of civil rights. Its first section reads: "Neither slavery nor involuntary servitude, except as a punishment for crime whereof the party shall have been duly convicted, shall exist within the United States, or any place subject to their jurisdiction."[4] Thus was slavery banned in the United States. Some 4 million African Americans who had lived in bondage were now free, but they were still not citizens of the United States with all the rights and privileges that accompany citizenship. Southern states took advantage of this situation by passing laws to deny blacks their proper role in a free society.

The Black Codes

In 1865 and 1866, southern states began passing legislation regulating the actions of former slaves. Called the Black Codes, these laws restricted African Americans' ability to own property or firearms, imposed harsh penalties for vagrancy (being unemployed or having a job not approved by whites), and barred them from work other than as farmhands. This last prohibition was designed to provide cheap labor to replace the slaves that had worked on southern plantations. Louisiana congressman Benjamin F. Flanders explained that these laws, which varied among the southern states, were aimed at "getting things back as near to slavery as possible."[5]

It was apparent to many in Congress that the rise of the Black Codes was proof that the Thirteenth Amendment alone would not prevent discrimination against African Americans. Illinois Senator Lyman Trumbull, who had coauthored the Thirteenth Amendment,

The Freedmen's Bureau

When 4 million African American slaves were given their freedom at the end of the Civil War, they were suddenly faced with many new challenges. The federal government stepped up to the task of helping the newly emancipated by establishing the Freedmen's Bureau in 1865.

Under the leadership of US Army general Oliver Howard, the bureau provided medical aid for millions of former slaves, distributed food and clothing to impoverished freedmen, and oversaw labor contracts between blacks and their former masters. Education was also an objective of the bureau, and it built some one thousand black schools. While these efforts helped ease the transition of many blacks from slavery to freedom, the bureau was not as successful in the area of civil rights.

Aware that African Americans could not receive fair trials in the states of the former Confederacy, the bureau set up its own courts. But these courts were hampered by white opposition and the virulent racism of the South, where whites still felt they could cheat, steal from, or even kill a black person without consequence. One bureau official in Mississippi asserted that whites "could not conceive of the negro having any rights at all."

The Freedmen's Bureau was dissolved in 1872, in part due to southern political pressure. While the bureau achieved some of its goals in helping former slaves, it could not create lasting advances in the civil rights of those who needed them the most.

Quoted in Eric Foner, *Reconstruction: America's Unfinished Revolution, 1863–1877*. New York: Harper & Row, 1988, p. 150.

introduced a bill in Congress in 1866 with the intent of abolishing the Black Codes. Trumbull told Congress, "When it comes to be understood in all parts of the United States that any person who shall deprive another of any right or subject him to any punishment in consequence of his color or race will expose himself to fine and imprisonment, I think such acts will soon cease."[6]

President Andrew Johnson, who had succeeded Lincoln after his assassination, vetoed Trumbull's bill, partly on the grounds that it infringed on the rights of white citizens. But on April 9, 1866, Congress overrode Johnson's veto and passed the legislation, which became the Civil Rights Act of 1866. The act granted citizenship to anyone born on US soil (including African Americans but not Native Americans), and affirmed that those citizens enjoy the same rights afforded to whites, such as the right to sue, engage in contracts, purchase property, and receive equal treatment under the law.

The passage of the Civil Rights Act of 1866 rendered the Black Codes illegal. Despite penalties outlined in the act, however, discrimination and violence against African Americans in the South continued.

Terror in the South

With the post-Civil War South in turmoil, fear among whites that freedmen would rebel against their former masters prompted the establishment of several white supremacist groups. Formed during Reconstruction, these groups began a reign of terror and intimidation against blacks. The most prominent group was the Ku Klux Klan, founded by Confederate veterans in 1866. Operating throughout the South, members of the KKK disguised themselves with white robes and hoods, making nighttime horseback raids on black communities. Klansmen burned schools and houses, beat, kidnapped, and lynched innocent blacks, and terrorized those who tried to register to vote. "In effect," says historian Eric Foner, "the Klan was a military force serving the interests of . . . all those who desired the restoration of white supremacy."[7] Local officials in the South wrote their state governors pleading for help to stem the growing violence.

> "The Klan was a military force serving the interests of . . . all those who desired the restoration of white supremacy."[7]
>
> —Historian Eric Foner

Frightened black citizens also wrote to voice their fears. "The ku kluks clan," read one letter to North Carolina governor William W. Holden, "is shooting our familys and beating them notoriously. We do not know what to do."[8]

Many governors responded by establishing militias to deal with the KKK and similar organizations. Thousands of Klansmen were arrested, tried, and imprisoned for their crimes, while others

A lithograph portrays members of the Ku Klux Klan in 1868. The white supremacist group was formed after the Civil War by Confederate army veterans who wanted to intimidate the freed slaves.

fled the South to avoid prosecution. As the white supremacist groups gradually began losing their power, Congress continued to define the rights of the freedmen through legislation.

More Rights for Freedmen

During Reconstruction, two more amendments were added to the Constitution. The Fourteenth Amendment, which was adopted on July 9, 1868, gave constitutional force to the provisions of the Civil Rights Act of 1866. The first section of the amendment guarantees the citizenship of any person who is born in

Death and Destruction in the Land of Lincoln

Springfield, Illinois, was the home of Abraham Lincoln, whose dedication to ending slavery and preserving the Union has made him one of America's most revered presidents. In an irony of history, Springfield was also the scene of a violent race riot that tarnished the reputation of Lincoln's hometown.

The seeds of the riot were planted with the jailing of two black men: Joe James, for murdering a white man, and George Richardson, accused of assaulting a white woman. On the afternoon of August 14, 1908, a crowd of angry white men gathered in front of the jail where the accused had been taken. Demanding that they be handed over for instant "justice," (that is, lynching), the mob became enraged when it learned that James and Richardson had been secretly moved to a jail in another town. Furious at being thwarted, the mob turned its anger on the African American citizens of Springfield.

In three days of violence a mob of some five thousand attacked Springfield's black business district, looting and destroying black-owned shops. The crowd then moved to the black neighborhood called the Badlands, burning down as many homes as they could. In the end, the Springfield riot resulted in at least seven deaths and property damage that would equal $3 million in today's currency.

But the riot had one positive legacy. The violence that wracked Springfield spurred the creation of the NAACP in 1909, the oldest and largest civil rights organization in America.

the United States or naturalized. In addition, it declares that no state may "deprive any person of life, liberty, or property, without due process of law; nor deny to any person within its jurisdiction the equal protection of the laws."[9] This provision is known as the Equal Protection Clause, and by prohibiting the states from legal discrimination, it has remained central to preserving the civil rights of all US citizens, regardless of race.

While the Fourteenth Amendment guaranteed citizenship, another important civil right was in need of constitutional protection: the right to vote. The second section of the amendment imposed the penalty of reducing the number of representatives in Congress for states that barred any citizen from voting. But this was a minor consequence and provided little deterrent to states that wished to enact restrictive voting laws. To ensure that all citizens were allowed by law to vote, Congress passed the Fifteenth Amendment on February 26, 1869, and it became officially a part of the Constitution on February 3, 1870. The Fifteenth Amendment states that "the right of citizens of the United States to vote shall not be denied or abridged by the United States or by any State on account of race, color, or previous condition of servitude."[10]

Abolitionist and journalist William Lloyd Garrison praised the new amendment by stating, "Nothing in all history equaled this wonderful, quiet, sudden transformation of four millions of human beings from . . . the auction block to the ballot-box."[11] The three Reconstruction-era amendments secured the civil rights that African Americans had been denied for generations. But the fight to hold on to those rights was far from over. As an 1871 editorial in an Illinois newspaper observed: "The negro is now a voter and a citizen. Let him hereafter take his chances in the battle of life."[12]

> "Nothing in all history equaled this wonderful, quiet, sudden transformation of four millions of human beings from . . . the auction block to the ballot-box."[11]
>
> —Journalist William Lloyd Garrison

The Beginning of Segregation

By 1877, all the former Confederate states had reentered the Union. Americans, both in the North and the South, were weary of the turmoil of the Reconstruction years, and concern for African American rights gradually faded. For a time it seemed that citizenship for African Americans was paying dividends; they were able to vote, and some held elected office. Blacks used the same railroads, parks, and other public accommodations as whites. But before long, governments sympathetic to white opposition against black progress regained hold in the southern states. Discrimination could once again flourish under state government approval.

In 1939, a black man drinks water at a segregated water fountain in a train terminal in Oklahoma. Established in 1881, the Jim Crow laws required separate public facilities for nonwhite people.

One consequence of that atmosphere was the enacting of oppressive legislation called Jim Crow laws, named for a black minstrel show character portrayed by a white actor in blackface makeup. First put into effect around 1881, Jim Crow laws were designed to separate people by race. The laws prohibited blacks from sharing with whites the same streetcars, schools, railroad stations, parks, and other public accommodations. Blacks could only use services specifically set aside for them.

On June 7, 1892, an African American named Homer Plessy boarded a whites-only railroad car in New Orleans. Under a Louisiana law called the Separate Car Act, Plessy was legally prohibited from riding in the same car as whites. When he re-fused to move to a blacks-only car, he was arrested and jailed.

Believing that his Fourteenth Amendment rights were violated, Plessy took his case to court. Found guilty by the Louisiana court, the case was appealed to the US Supreme Court in 1896. In the landmark case of *Plessy v. Ferguson*, the court ruled that by providing "separate but equal" accommodations for African American passengers, the railroad did not violate the Fourteenth Amendment. With this decision, the highest court in the United States declared that racial segregation did not violate the Constitution, essentially confirming that African Americans were, indeed, second-class citizens.

Organizing the Opposition

Less-than-full citizenship angered African American leaders, who began to work toward restoring the civil rights that had been taken away by unscrupulous southern legislators. Among those leaders was Booker T. Washington, who was born into slavery in 1856. Washington had founded the Tuskegee Institute in Alabama to provide vocational education to southern blacks. He believed that the way to advance his race was by teaching skills that would make blacks indispensable to the South's economy, thereby becoming respectable members of society. In 1895, Washington negotiated an agreement, called the Atlanta Compromise, with southern leaders. In return for receiving vocational education, blacks would not stage protests or demonstrate for equality.

Many African American leaders opposed Washington's idea, saying that it amounted to accepting segregation and discrimination. One young man, W.E.B. DuBois, spearheaded a movement that encouraged blacks to fight for what was rightfully theirs. Born in a mostly white, middle-class town in Massachusetts, DuBois was well-educated, having earned a doctorate from Harvard University in 1890. In 1905, DuBois organized the Niagara Movement, a group of African Americans dedicated to fighting for black civil rights. In a speech DuBois wrote for the organization's first public meeting in August 1906, he defined the Niagara Movement's goal:

> Against this [discrimination] the Niagara Movement eternally protests. We will not be satisfied to take one jot or tittle less than our full manhood rights. We claim for ourselves every single right that belongs to a freeborn American, political, civil and social; and until we get these rights we will never cease to protest and assail the ears of America.[13]

As an alternative to Washington's philosophy of accommodation, the Niagara Movement was the beginning of activism in the securing of civil rights. Although it was always underfunded and lasted only four years, the Niagara Movement was the forerunner of the oldest and most influential civil rights organization in the United States: the National Association for the Advancement of Colored People (NAACP).

The NAACP

The NAACP was established in 1909, partly in response to a massive race riot in Springfield, Illinois, the previous year. Founding members of the organization included civil rights activist and journalist Oswald Garrison Villard, journalist Mary White Ovington, and W.E.B. DuBois. Headquartered in New York, the NAACP included both blacks and whites in its membership. Its official publication, the *Crisis*, was founded by DuBois as a platform for discussing issues of African American interest.

The NAACP filed lawsuits against segregation and limitations on voting rights. It also advocated for African American participation in the armed forces during World War I. In 1915, when *Birth of a Nation*, a Hollywood movie glorifying the KKK was released, the NAACP staged a largely unsuccessful nationwide effort to have the film banned. More successful was its campaign against lynching. Under its auspices, a group of African American women formed the Anti-Lynching Crusaders. The group protested lynchings by writing newspaper articles, organizing protests, and raising money to petition Congress to pass an anti-lynching bill. Although it failed to get the law passed, the Crusaders' actions brought the problem to the American public's attention, and the group's efforts are usually considered a prime cause of the gradual decline in the crime.

By 1919, the NAACP had some ninety thousand members. Throughout the next three decades, little progress was made in the struggle for civil rights. The US military, however, became a leader in racial integration. In 1941, with World War II on the horizon, President Franklin D. Roosevelt required the desegregation of the defense industry, which produced weapons for the impending conflict. In 1948, Roosevelt's successor, Harry S. Truman, ordered the US armed forces, which had fought the war mostly with segregated units, to henceforth offer "equality of treatment and opportunity for all persons in the armed services without regard to race, color, religion or national origin."[14]

Despite all the efforts made on behalf of African American civil rights, blacks in America continued to bear the stigma of second-class citizenship. Jim Crow was still the law of the land in the South. On trains and buses, in schools, at parks, and in theaters, the world of the African American was one of separation and humiliation, defined by signs that proclaimed "Whites Only." But by the middle of the twentieth century, the movement seeking justice and equality for African Americans finally began to gain momentum.

> "We claim for ourselves every single right that belongs to a freeborn American, political, civil and social; and until we get these rights we will never cease to protest and assail the ears of America."[13]
>
> —Civil rights activist W.E.B DuBois

CHAPTER TWO

Demonstrating for Equality

The F.W. Woolworth store in Greensboro, North Carolina, was typical of the "five-and-dime" stores that were popular in the mid-twentieth century. Forerunner of modern discount chains, Woolworth stores featured a variety of consumer goods, and most had a lunch counter where shoppers could relax over a sandwich and a soda. On the afternoon of February 1, 1960, four students from North Carolina Agriculture and Technical College (A&T) sat down at the Greensboro Woolworth's lunch counter and asked to be served. The waitress behind the counter declined their request, saying, "I'm sorry. We don't serve Negroes here."[15]

Despite this refusal, the A&T students remained at the counter until the store closed. They returned the next day, accompanied by thirty more students. Again refused service, the students did not complain or damage store property; they simply opened books and started reading to pass the time. By the end of the week, media coverage of this "sit-in" had inspired similar protests across the South. Six months later, the lunch counter at the Greensboro Woolworth was desegregated. The victory showed the power of a peaceful protest to effect social change. Ezell Blair Jr., one of the original four students, later recalled, "We didn't want to put the world on fire, we just wanted to eat. . . . We were hoping it would catch on and it would spread throughout the country, but it went even beyond our wildest imagination."[16]

> "We didn't want to put the world on fire, we just wanted to eat."[16]
>
> —Sit-in activist Ezell Blair Jr.

The sit-in became one of the most widespread methods of protest during the Civil Rights Movement of the 1960s. And in the segregated South, there was much to protest.

Life and Death in the Segregated South

As the United States entered the decade of the 1950s, Jim Crow was still alive in the South and in much of the North as well. In the South there were, in fact, two societies: one for whites and one for blacks, and the southern whites did everything they could to keep the two separated. An African American from Austin, Texas, recalls the pain of growing up under Jim Crow:

> Jim Crow really hurt. As a rural child, we thought it was stupid when we first began to be aware of it. . . . As we grew, we noticed the separate drinking fountains, restrooms and waiting areas. The white ones were always cleaner and nicer than the colored. The colored didn't even have separate restrooms for men and women, and I saw one such that was really filthy, whereas the white one I had been taken to was clean. It didn't make sense, but it was cruel.[17]

Ministers picket outside the F.W. Woolworth store in Greensboro, North Carolina. Many were outraged by the store's policy of not serving black people.

Segregation was not only cruel for blacks in physical terms, such as being required to use separate restrooms, but psychologically as well. Jim Crow affected even the most basic social conventions. African Americans were obliged to address whites using the title Mr. or Mrs. as an indication that they were speaking to someone of superior status. Whites, on the other hand, referred to blacks by their first names; when a name was not known, the belittling terms "boy," "girl," or "uncle" were used. Blacks were expected to use the back door to enter a white person's house.

One Youth's Perspective on Marching

The thousands of people who marched for civil rights represented a diversity of races, genders, religions, and ages. Many were young adults who, for the first time, had found a cause behind which they could put their energies and beliefs. One young activist was Myrna Carter, who writes about one of the many marches she participated in:

I remember one march very well. We met at New Pilgrim Church [in Birmingham] that Sunday. Immediately after the service we lined up in two's to march to Memorial Park, directly across from the City Police Department. This particular Sunday we had children and people of all ages. When we got to Memorial Park, [police chief] Bull Connor was there. The Birmingham fire department was all ready with their hoses. The hose was so long, they had a line of firemen holding it every few feet. And the policemen were there with their dogs. The dogs were on leashes. They'd lunge and the police would pull them back. They thought it was funny to let them almost get to us. We were afraid of the dogs, but we were not to show fear. We were to keep walking and singing as if they were not there.

When we got to Memorial Park, Reverend Billups was standing in front of the group, and he said, "We are ready for your fire hoses, your dogs, and anything else!" And tears just started running down his face. I'll never forget it.

Quoted in Ellen Levine, *Freedom's Children: Young Civil Rights Activists Tell Their Own Stories*. New York: Puffin, 2000, p. 88.

When walking down a street, African Americans had to step off the sidewalk to let whites pass.

African American men had to be especially careful when in the presence of a white woman. In the Jim Crow era, even an innocent look or harmless word could be interpreted by whites as an improper advance by a black toward a white woman, often leading to tragic consequences. In August 1955, a black fourteen-year-old from Chicago named Emmett Till was in Mississippi visiting relatives. Acting on a dare from some friends, Till allegedly spoke to and, according to some accounts whistled at, a white woman at a grocery store. Upon hearing of the teen's actions, the woman's husband and his half-brother kidnapped, tortured, and murdered Till, dumping his body in a nearby river.

The two men were subsequently arrested and tried for the murder. Their acquittal by an all-white jury led to demonstrations in Baltimore, Chicago, Detroit, New York, and other cities. There was extensive print and broadcast coverage of the murder and trial, prompting historian David Halberstam to call the incident "the first great media event of the Civil Rights Movement."[18] Editorials such as the following from the magazine *Commonweal* regarded Till's murder as a call to action:

> By his death Emmett Louis Till took racism out of the textbooks and showed it to the world in its true dimensions. Now the ugliness is there for all the world to see. In the face of this, what can decent men do except redouble their efforts to cure ourselves of this evil thing?[19]

The "evil thing" that segregation had created was about to be challenged by courageous people in the streets, at the workplace, and on public transportation. Three months after Emmett Till was laid to rest, an African American seamstress named Rosa Parks stepped onto a bus and into the forefront of the Civil Rights Movement.

Boycotting Buses

Jim Crow laws in Montgomery, Alabama, required African Americans to ride in the rear section of the city buses. If a white passenger was unable to find a seat, a black passenger had to relinquish his or her seat and stand for the duration of the ride.

On December 1, 1955, forty-two-year-old Rosa Parks boarded a bus after work and sat down in the middle of the bus, in the first row of the segregated black section. The bus was half full, but as more white passengers got on, the driver told the black passengers in Parks's row to move back. The other passengers complied, but Parks remained in her seat, challenging the driver's authority. The driver summoned police, who arrested Parks, charging her with violation of Montgomery's segregation laws.

Parks was no stranger to the struggle for civil rights. She was the secretary of the Alabama State Conference of the NAACP and had attended a training session for civil rights activists the previous year. She later explained the reason behind her decision to remain in her seat that day:

> "People always say that I didn't give up my seat because I was tired, but that isn't true. . . . There had to be a stopping place, and this seemed to have been the place for me to stop being pushed around."[20]
>
> —Bus boycott pioneer Rosa Parks

People always say that I didn't give up my seat because I was tired, but that isn't true. I was not tired physically, or no more tired than I usually was at the end of a working day. . . . No, the only tired I was, was tired of giving in. . . . There had to be a stopping place, and this seemed to have been the place for me to stop being pushed around.[20]

Later that day, Parks was bailed out of jail by prominent black leader E.D. Nixon, and a court date was set for Monday, December 5. Around the same time, JoAnn Robinson, a college professor and member of the civil rights organization Women's Political

Council, was planning a one-day boycott of the Montgomery City Bus Lines in protest of Parks's arrest. Robinson spent the night of December 2 printing thirty-five thousand handbills urging the African American population of Montgomery to avoid riding buses on Monday. Nixon and a group of black ministers meeting that same night endorsed the idea of a boycott.

On Monday, while Parks was found guilty and fined fourteen dollars, the bus boycott began. Most of Montgomery's African American riders avoided riding the buses, opting instead to walk, ride a bicycle, take a taxi, or simply stay home for the day. The one-day boycott was so successful—90 percent of Montgomery's black population participated—that it was decided to continue it until the city desegregated its buses. An organization called the Montgomery Improvement Association (MIA) was formed to keep

Rosa Parks is fingerprinted at the county jail in Montgomery, Alabama, after her arrest in 1955. Parks was arrested for not giving up her bus seat to a white passenger.

the boycott going. The group organized carpools to help with transportation to jobs, provided assistance to boycotters who lost their jobs, and held regular meetings to keep interest in the boycott from flagging. To head the organization as its president, the MIA chose a little-known local pastor, twenty-six-year-old Martin Luther King Jr.

What started as a one-day protest lasted 381 days, ending on December 20, 1956. The US Supreme Court upheld a lower court's finding that Montgomery's bus laws were unconstitutional under the Fourteenth Amendment. With that decision, blacks no longer had to sit in segregated sections of the buses. The Montgomery bus boycott showed that the power of economic pressure could bring about eventual change. It demonstrated that ordinary African Americans could organize a peaceful protest to obtain their goals, even if some of those goals were not immediately realized in an era of Jim Crow discrimination. For example, even though many southern blacks still stayed seated in the rear of buses because they feared retaliation, media coverage of the boycott raised national awareness of the black struggle for equality.

As peaceful as the boycott was, however, white reaction to it was anything but. Black pedestrians walking to work or school were verbally taunted and pelted with rotten eggs. The homes of King and Nixon were bombed. Such reactions showed that fighting for equality in the South was still a slow and dangerous undertaking—a situation that sympathetic protesters from the North would soon find out.

Freedom Riders

Growing up in Appleton, Wisconsin, James Zwerg had little contact with African Americans in the nearly all-white community. But as a twenty-one-year-old college student on May 17, 1961, Zwerg sat on a Greyhound bus as it left Nashville, Tennessee, heading south, its destination New Orleans, Louisiana. Of the ten people on the bus, Zwerg was one of only two whites. The group, known as the Freedom Riders, was on its way to protest

Medgar Evers: Murder in Mississippi

Medgar Evers was an African American who served honorably in the US Army during World War II. After the war, Evers was appointed the first NAACP field secretary in Mississippi. One of his first tasks was to investigate the murder of Emmett Till.

Evers knew that working for civil rights in Mississippi was dangerous, especially for a high-profile member of the NAACP. In the 1960s, whenever he drove to or from a meeting, Evers was followed by white supremacists. On June 12, 1963, Evers arrived at his home in Jackson, Mississippi, just after midnight and parked in his driveway. As he walked toward his house a shot rang out, the bullet striking Evers in the back. He was able to crawl almost to the front door when he collapsed. Rushed to a local hospital, he died an hour later. Medgar Evers was thirty-seven years old.

White supremacist Byron De La Beckwith, a local salesman, was charged with the murder, but all-white juries twice found him not guilty. Feeling safe from further prosecution, Beckwith often hinted that he did, in fact, kill Evers. After thirty years, new evidence emerged, and another trial was conducted in 1994. This time, a jury of eight blacks and four whites found Beckwith guilty. He died in prison in 2001.

Evers is often quoted as saying, "You can kill a man, but you can't kill an idea." Evers lived and died for the idea that civil rights were for everyone.

Quoted in Herb Boyd, *We Shall Overcome*. Naperville, IL: Sourcebooks, 2004, p. 145.

the segregation of interstate bus terminals in the southern states. The protest was organized by the Congress of Racial Equality (CORE), a multiracial civil rights group, whose leaders knew that the trip would be dangerous. But for Zwerg, who was planning a career in the ministry, it was something that had to be done. "I was never so certain of something in my life,"[21] he later recalled.

The journey was not the first Freedom Ride. On May 4, another group with the same task had headed south from Washington, DC. But in Birmingham, Alabama, a mob attacked the group, severely beating the Freedom Riders and setting fire to their bus. What could have been the end of the Freedom Rides became motivation for the second group to continue the mission. As the Greyhound carrying Zwerg and the other riders rolled into Montgomery, Alabama, the streets were quiet. When they left the bus, however, groups of angry whites began pouring out of nearby buildings. With metal pipes, baseball bats, and other makeshift weapons, the mob advanced on the Freedom Riders. An eyewitness reported, "A bunch of men . . . are beating them. There are no cops. It's terrible. It's terrible. There's not a cop in sight. People are yelling, 'Get 'em, get 'em.' It's awful."[22]

As one of the two whites, Zwerg, reviled by the mob as a white sympathizer, got the worst of the beatings. He was kicked, punched, and thrown over a railing. Other riders, including John Lewis, a black civil rights activist who had befriended Zwerg in Nashville, were also beaten. Only after Alabama state troopers and local police arrived did the violence subside.

Images of a battered and bruised Zwerg lying in the hospital appeared in newspapers and on television. But the Freedom Riders would not be defeated. In a statement from his hospital bed Zwerg said, "Segregation must be stopped. It must be broken down. . . . We're going on to New Orleans no matter what happens. We're dedicated to this. We'll take hitting. We'll take beating. We're willing to accept death."[23]

> "Segregation must be stopped. It must be broken down. . . . We're dedicated to this. We'll take hitting. We'll take beating. We're willing to accept death."[23]
>
> —Freedom Rider James Zwerg

Between May and September 1961, some sixty Freedom Rides took place throughout the South, involving more than 430 riders. During these rides, beatings continued, and concern about the violence eventually reached the highest levels of government. President Kennedy tried to persuade Alabama governor John Patterson to provide protection for the protesters, but Patterson refused. After one particularly brutal encounter between the riders and local whites, federal marshals were sent to Montgomery to try to prevent further violence.

As a result of the Freedom Rides, in November 1961, the Interstate Commerce Commission outlawed segregation in interstate transportation. In bus stations and railroad terminals across the South "Whites Only" and "Colored Only" signs came down.

The Freedom Riders gave a new momentum to the Civil Rights Movement, inspiring others—both white and black—to join the growing effort for equality. In a televised speech on June 11, 1963, Kennedy urged Congress to pass a new civil rights bill. Journalist Evan Thomas later remarked that there was a "direct line from the Freedom Riders to the speech that President Kennedy gave in June of 1963."[24] The bill eventually became the Civil Rights Act of 1964.

Marching on Washington

Eleven days after Kennedy delivered his civil rights speech, he was sitting in the White House Cabinet Room with King and five other African American activists. The day before, civil rights leaders had officially announced their plans for one hundred thousand people to gather in Washington, DC, to demonstrate "for jobs and freedom." Kennedy was concerned that a violent response to the march could jeopardize his civil rights bill. The men ultimately convinced the president that, since the march was being organized by leaders experienced in nonviolent demonstrations, such risks would be minimized. The march was set for August 28, 1963, in the middle of the sweltering Washington summer.

Marchers began gathering in the early morning hours of August 28—men and women, black and white, young and old, ordinary folks and celebrities. They carried signs and sang protest songs, marching past National Guardsmen and Washington Metropolitan Police officers stationed along the way. By midday, more than two hundred thousand marchers had assembled along the Washington Mall and on the steps of the Lincoln Memorial. After a morning of speeches by civil rights leaders and songs by gospel and folk singers, the crowd was growing weary in the oppressive heat. The last speaker of the day, King, finally stepped up to the lectern and began what would become the most famous speech of the Civil Rights Movement.

Reading from a prepared text, King's voice was strong, but as he spoke he sensed that the crowd's attention was wandering.

With the throng before him and television cameras broadcasting to a nationwide audience, King put aside his script and began to passionately speak about his dream. Clarence Jones, who helped write King's prepared text, was behind King. "I said to somebody standing next to me: 'These people don't know it, but they're about to go to church.' I said that because I could see his body language change from the rear. Where he had been reading, like giving a lecture, but then going into his Baptist preacher mode."[25]

Martin Luther King Jr. acknowledges the crowd in Washington, DC, before he gives what would become the most famous speech of the Civil Rights Movement. King spoke of his dream of equality for people of all colors.

King spoke eloquently of his dream of equality for people of all colors. "I have a dream," King said, "that my four little children will one day live in a nation where they will not be judged by the color of their skin but by the content of their character." King concluded his message with the words of an old Negro spiritual: "Free at last! Free at last! Thank God Almighty, we are free at last!"[26] The crowd thundered its approval with cheers and applause. Kennedy, who watched the speech on television in the Oval Office, later expressed his admiration for King's message.

> "Free at last! Free at last! Thank God Almighty, we are free at last!"[26]
>
> —Dr. Martin Luther King Jr.

The marchers departed Washington as peacefully as they had come, and by evening the city had returned to normal. Kennedy later called the march, "one of the biggest, most creative and constructive demonstrations ever held in the history of our nation."[27] His fears of the march having negative effects on his civil rights bill turned out to be unfounded. But he did not live to see the bill become law. Less than three months after the March on Washington, Kennedy was assassinated in Dallas, Texas. Lyndon B. Johnson, Kennedy's successor, ultimately guided the bill through Congress, and on July 2, 1964, signed it into law. The Civil Rights Act of 1964 banned discrimination in public places and guaranteed equality in job opportunities, one of the March on Washington's primary goals.

King, as the most influential civil rights leader, advocated a nonviolent approach to fighting racial discrimination. Peaceful demonstrations such as the sit-ins, boycotts, and marches of the 1960s became the backbone of, and the power behind, the Civil Rights Movement.

CHAPTER THREE

Ending School Segregation

It was the fall of 1950, and Barbara Rose Johns was fed up. The fifteen-year-old student at Robert R. Moton High School in Farmville, Virginia, was tired of conditions at the segregated school. Built to accommodate fewer than 200 students, the school now held 450. Three ugly tar-paper shacks had been added to the original building to handle the overcrowding. Moton had no cafeteria, no gym, and no locker room for the sports teams. Barbara knew that white schools in the area had much better facilities, and she was angry that promised improvements to Moton had not materialized.

In October, Barbara met with four other students to discuss the problem. Barbara suggested that if the school board did not remedy the situation, they would call for a student strike. On April 23, 1951, after the school board had failed to act, Barbara summoned the student body to gather in the auditorium. Barbara's sister Joan recalls that morning:

> When the curtains opened it was my sister on stage rather than the principal. I was totally shocked. She stood up there and addressed the school. She seemed to have everyone's attention. . . . At one point, she took off her shoe and she banged on the podium and said that we were going to go out on strike and would everyone please cooperate and "don't be afraid, just follow us out." So we did. The entire student body followed her out.[28]

The student strike at Moton High School lasted two weeks. During that time, Barbara and the other strike leaders met with lawyers from the NAACP who filed a lawsuit on behalf of the Moton students to request the repeal of the school district's segregation laws. Named for one of the students, *Davis v. County School Board of Prince Edward County*, was rejected by the court. That rejection was not the end, but the beginning of the fight for integrated schools. The case would become part of the landmark US Supreme Court case *Brown v. Board of Education*, which ended school segregation in the United States.

The Beginning of *Brown*

Across the segregated South, black students were forced to walk or ride buses for long distances to their schools, even though a white school was closer. Linda Brown, a black student in Topeka, Kansas, had to cross a busy highway and walk through a dangerous railroad yard to catch a bus for her half-hour ride to school. The local white school was only four blocks from her house. Linda's father, Oliver Brown, was angry that his daughter had to go so far to attend a segregated school. "Why should my child walk four miles when there is a school only four blocks away?"[29] Linda remembers him saying. Around this time, John Scott, a lawyer

Monroe Elementary school in Topeka, Kansas, has been established as a national historic site. In 1950, Oliver Brown tried to enroll his black daughter at the white school that was only a few blocks from their house.

with the Topeka NAACP, was looking for families to participate in a legal challenge of school segregation. Scott asked Brown to try to enroll Linda in the white school, knowing that the attempt would fail. When it did, it became the basis for an appeal to the US Supreme Court, along with *Davis* and three other cases from across the nation that had had the same outcome. The combined lawsuit would thrust the Brown family name into civil rights history.

Thurgood Marshall Challenges Segregation

If there was any lawyer that could successfully shepherd the *Brown* case through the nation's legal system, it was Thurgood Marshall. Born in 1908 in Baltimore, Maryland, young Marshall had a mischievous personality. In high school, he learned the Constitution by

The Doll Tests

Among the evidence Thurgood Marshall presented before the Supreme Court in *Brown v. Board of Education* were the findings of a test given to sixteen black children, ages six to nine, by psychologists Kenneth B. Clark and his wife, Mamie. The test was designed to determine how these children understood and expressed their racial identity, and it was conducted at Marshall's request in South Carolina. The test duplicated tests that the Clarks had performed nationwide in the 1940s.

The Clarks used two dolls, identical except for their color: one doll was white with yellow hair and the other was brown with black hair. The children were asked questions about the dolls, such as whether a doll was "nice" or "bad," which one they would like to play with, and which doll looked most like themselves. The majority of the children expressed a preference for the white dolls and associated positive attributes with them, while rejecting the brown dolls. In court, Marshall presented the results as scientific evidence that living in a segregated environment harms a black child's self-identity and sense of worth.

In 2005, the doll test was duplicated for a documentary film made by sixteen-year-old film student Kiri Davis, who gave the test to black children from Harlem in New York City. Again, most of the children preferred the white doll over the brown one. Davis's experiment showed that despite fifty years of civil rights progress, racial discrimination continues to negatively affect black children.

heart, a result of being punished for his frequent mischief in class by having to memorize a passage while banished to the school's basement. One part of the Constitution that especially inspired him was the Fourteenth Amendment's guarantee of equal rights for all. After graduating from Lincoln University in Pennsylvania, Marshall entered the all-black Howard University Law School in Washington, DC, graduating first in his class in 1933.

As a lawyer, Marshall could now help fight discrimination against African Americans, specifically the "separate but equal" decision of *Plessy v. Ferguson*. In 1936, he joined the NAACP as a staff lawyer, and in 1940 he created the NAACP's Legal Defense and Educational Fund (LDF) to pursue litigation in civil rights cases. Years of civil rights lawsuits paved the way for Marshall and his team of lawyers to finally mount a challenge to segregation before the US Supreme Court.

Brown v. Board of Education

On December 9, 1952, the nine black-robed justices of the US Supreme Court filed into the courtroom. Lawyers for the five combined cases in *Brown v. Board of Education* took their places and, around 1:30 p.m., began pleading their cases. For the next three days, the lawyers argued that segregated schools were detrimental to the development of African American children. Marshall cited studies conducted by experts that concluded that "segregation deterred the development of the personalities of these [black] children. . . . that it deprives them of equal status in the school community, that it destroys their self-respect."[30] Marshall then added a personal note:

> I know in the South where I spent most of my time, you will see white and colored kids going down the road together to school. They separate and go to different schools, and they come out and they play together. I do not see why there would necessarily be any trouble if they went to school together.[31]

After all the lawyers' arguments on both sides had been heard, the court adjourned on December 11, and the wait for the justices to deliberate and reach a decision began. It would be a long wait. The justices were divided on how to rule: some were in favor of preserving segregation, while others felt that it should be abolished. A new court date was set for October 1953 but was delayed when Chief Justice Fred Vinson died in September, and Earl Warren, his replacement, had to familiarize himself with his new position.

On December 7, 1953, the Supreme Court reconvened to hear the lawyers argue their cases once more. After another three days filled with arguments and rebuttals, the court adjourned on December 9. It would be five months before a decision was announced. On Monday, May 17, 1954, Chief Justice Warren read the opinion of the court: "We conclude that in the field of public education the doctrine of 'separate but equal' has no place. Separate educational facilities are inherently unequal."[32]

> "We conclude that in the field of public education the doctrine of 'separate but equal' has no place. Separate educational facilities are inherently unequal."[32]
>
> —Chief Justice of the United States Earl Warren

After fifty-eight years of inequality for African Americans, *Plessy v. Ferguson* was overturned. That afternoon, Marshall and his colleagues held a jubilant party to celebrate the historic victory. As the party continued into the night and the euphoria of the victory began to fade, Marshall's mood grew subdued. "I don't want any of you to fool yourselves," he said to his celebrating staff, "it's just begun, the fight has just begun."[33]

Backlash

As Marshall had expected, not everyone was happy with the Supreme Court's decision in *Brown*. At the time of the decision, school segregation was required in seventeen states and allowed in four more. Almost immediately after the *Brown* decision, many governors of those states began to fight the desegregation of their schools. Many simply refused to comply with the law. Oth-

Thurgood Marshall, center, celebrates with colleagues outside the US Supreme Court in 1954. The court ruled in their favor, concluding that school segregation was unconstitutional.

ers closed schools rather than see them integrated. Some white families packed up and moved to the suburbs to avoid sending their children to city schools that would eventually be integrated.

Although the *Brown* decision had mandated desegregation, it did not specify how that was to be accomplished. In 1955, the Supreme Court heard another case (also titled *Brown v. Board of Education*, but usually referred to as *Brown II)* to address that problem. The court's decision instructed the states to implement desegregation "with all deliberate speed." The vagueness of that phrase helped the southern states, whose governors could delay desegregation almost indefinitely while claiming that they were working toward compliance with "deliberate speed." In the

Integrating Ole Miss

James Meredith wanted to go to college. Born in 1933 in Kosciusko, Mississippi, Meredith attended segregated schools in Mississippi and Florida, graduating from high school in 1951. At the time, segregationist sentiment and his lack of funds forced him to postpone his dream of higher education. He enlisted in the US Air Force and performed two tours of duty in the United States and Japan.

Upon leaving the Air Force in 1960, Meredith moved back to Mississippi. He believed education was the key to fighting racism, so he enrolled at Jackson State College, a black college. There he met other blacks interested in civil rights, and he joined the NAACP. While Meredith was in the Air Force, *Brown v. Board of Education* had mandated school desegregation. He felt it was time to test that ruling, so in 1961 he applied to the University of Mississippi, commonly known as Ole Miss. After two rejections, Meredith and the NAACP filed a lawsuit claiming Meredith was denied entrance to the university solely because of his race. Meredith ultimately won his case and was scheduled to enter Ole Miss in September 1962. US Attorney General Robert Kennedy ordered fifty US marshals to accompany Meredith on his first days. Although harassment of Meredith continued, he eventually graduated in 1963 with a degree in political science.

meantime, the media predicted dire consequences in the wake of *Brown*. "Human blood may stain southern soil in many places because of this decision," proclaimed an editorial in the *Jacksonville (NC) News*. The *Jackson (MS) Daily News* said of the decision, "It means racial strife of the bitterest sort."[34] A resident of Montgomery, Alabama, made an ominous prediction after his city desegregated its buses in 1956: "Now this school mixing stuff, that'll be coming next . . . that's sure where we're gonna draw our line."[35] Soon, such a line would be drawn around a Little Rock, Arkansas, high school that was about to be integrated.

Crisis at Central High

Built in 1927, Little Rock Central High School is an outstanding example of Collegiate Gothic architecture, and shortly after its construction it was named "America's Most Beautiful High

School." Its striking white main entrance is adorned with four statues representing Ambition, Personality, Opportunity, and Preparation. At the school's dedication, Lillian McDermott of the school board proclaimed Central High "a public school where Ambition is fired, where Personality is developed, where Opportunity is presented and where Preparation in the solution of life's problems is begun."[36] But for its first thirty years, those advantages were available only to white students.

Segregation was the way of life in Arkansas, as it was in the rest of the South in the Jim Crow years. Central High was a whites-only school, until the *Brown* decision forced Arkansas school officials to devise a strategy for integrating its schools. The plan they developed called for high schools to be integrated first, followed later by junior high and elementary schools. A list of two hundred black students eligible to transfer was narrowed down until ten students (one would later decide not to change schools) were chosen to enter Central for the 1957–58 school year.

Preparing for Central High

The nine students, six girls and three boys, began preparations to enter their new school on September 4, 1957. Fourteen-year-old Carlotta Walls, the youngest of the nine, recalls making her decision to go to Central High:

> Central High, that grand building looming in the distance as I walked to school practically every day now would open its doors to me. I'd heard so much about it. . . . I couldn't help wondering how much wider my options for college would be if I attended Central and suddenly had all its resources available to me.[37]

Carlotta's excitement was not shared by all of the adults around her. "I couldn't understand," she remembers, "why all of my relatives weren't just thrilled that I was preparing to attend one of the top high schools in America."[38] What they knew was that integrating the school would be dangerous. As soon as desegregation was announced, white residents of the school district mounted a concerted effort to keep the African American students out of Central High. There were threats of violence against the black students and their relatives, and pro-segregation groups planned to block the new students from entering the school. Arkansas's governor, Orval Faubus, was on the side of the segregationists. In his campaign for governor, Faubus had declared, "No school district will be forced to mix the races as long as I am governor of Arkansas."[39] On September 2, 1957, the day before the fall semester was to begin, Faubus announced he would use the Arkansas National Guard to prevent the students from entering the school. The stage was set for a confrontation at Central High.

> "No school district will be forced to mix the races as long as I am governor of Arkansas."[39]
>
> —Arkansas governor Orval Faubus

The Little Rock Nine

On September 4, 1957, the nine students met at a corner a few blocks from Central High and, escorted by several white and African American ministers, began walking toward their new school. As they approached the building, a contingent of 250 Arkansas National Guardsmen and an angry crowd of white protesters confronted them. They made their way through the taunts and epithets hurled at them from the crowd. "I tried to see a friendly face somewhere in the mob," recalls Elizabeth Eckford. "I looked into the face of an old woman, and it seemed a kind face, but when I looked at her again, she spat on me."[40] When they reached the doors of the school, the Guardsmen refused to let them pass. Their attempt to enter Central High blocked, the

> "I tried to see a friendly face somewhere in the mob. I looked into the face of an old woman, and it seemed a kind face, but when I looked at her again, she spat on me."[40]
>
> —Central High School Student Elizabeth Eckford

African American students left the school grounds amid more jeers from the crowd.

On September 23, after several weeks of legal delays, the Little Rock Nine finally entered Little Rock Central High School through a side door, avoiding an angry mob of about one thousand at the main entrance. Meanwhile, at his vacation retreat in Newport, Rhode Island, President Dwight D. Eisenhower had been following the events unfolding at Central High. Aware of his duty to enforce the federal desegregation law, Eisenhower made a tough decision: he ordered the United States Army to ensure that the Little Rock Nine could safely continue to attend their new school.

On September 24, twelve hundred troops from the army's elite 101st Airborne Division took up positions in front of Central High, deploying jeeps, tents, and communication lines. The next morning the Little Rock Nine arrived for classes in a convoy protected by soldiers in jeeps. Once at the school, the soldiers escorted them inside. Despite a few incidents, the crowd had been silenced by the presence of the hardened combat troops in battle gear, bayonets gleaming on their rifles.

In 1957, US Army officers escort black students from Central High School in Little Rock, Arkansas. President Eisenhower ordered the army to ensure a peaceful desegregation of the school.

Aftermath

For the remainder of the school year, each of the nine students had a soldier assigned to them as a bodyguard. Although many white classmates continued making verbal and physical assaults, others befriended them; one girl, Minniejean Brown, was even invited to join the glee club. But when she was asked to sing a solo, a segregationist group, the Mothers' League, complained that black students "are not supposed to take part in things like that."[41] Some white students felt that their parents were the major cause of the troubles at Central High and that the violence would end if they stayed away.

On May 29, 1958, Ernest Green, the only senior of the nine, became the first African American to graduate from Little Rock Central High School. The others faced a tougher challenge to graduate. Governor Faubus closed all of Little Rock's schools for the 1958–59 school year to delay further desegregation. Some of the nine graduated from Central after it was reopened in 1959. Others completed their high school education by taking night or correspondence classes or graduating from other schools. Minniejean Brown was expelled from Central High for retaliating against a vicious taunt from a white student; she finished her high school education in New York City. All of the Little Rock Nine eventually earned college degrees.

The legacy of the Little Rock Nine is honored in the Little Rock Nine Memorial. Located on the grounds of the Arkansas State Capitol in Little Rock, the memorial, titled "Testament," consists of life-size bronze statues of the nine students, books in hand, on their way to school. But the larger legacy of these nine students lies in the impact their courage had on civil rights. Television news coverage of the crisis brought the issue of desegregation into America's living rooms. A little more than a week after the nine entered Central High, Little Rock Presbyterian minister Dunbar Ogden Jr. commented, "This may be looked back upon by future historians as the turning point—for good—of race relations in this country."[42] It is a turning point that stands with Rosa Parks and the Freedom Riders as a key milestone in the Civil Rights Movement.

CHAPTER FOUR

Securing the Right to Vote

Thomas Mundy Peterson, a forty-five-year-old African American and the son of a freed slave, worked as a school custodian in the town of Perth Amboy, New Jersey. On March 31, 1870, a local election was held to decide whether the town's charter should be revised or eliminated. "I was working for Mr. T. L. Kearny," Peterson later recalled, "[who] advised me to go to the polls and exercise a citizen's privilege."[43] When Peterson cast his ballot that day, he was making civil rights history. He was the first African American in the nation to vote under the newly ratified Fifteenth Amendment, which made it illegal to deny the right to vote to anyone "on account of race, color, or previous condition of servitude."[44]

Although some people were troubled by an African American voting—it is said that one white man tore up his ballot in protest—Peterson's act was generally respected by the townspeople; in 1884, the town awarded him a gold commemorative medallion for his action. Peterson may be considered fortunate that he lived in a northern state. In the South, barriers that prevented blacks from rightfully exercising their Fifteenth Amendment rights still existed.

Taxes and Tests

One method used by white southerners in the late nineteenth and early twentieth centuries to deny African Americans their right to vote was the poll tax. This tax had to be paid before a person could register to vote. Although it amounted to only a dollar or two, it was usually beyond the means of most poor blacks. The poll tax effectively disenfranchised, or excluded from voting, African Americans, who were left without a say in how their government was run. By 1908, every southern state imposed a poll tax.

Along with the poll tax, literacy tests were often required. These tests required prospective voters to answer numerous questions on government, US history, and other topics to test the person's knowledge. Passing the test was necessary to vote. Most blacks, who were denied an education during years of slavery, were at a decided disadvantage.

Although the literacy test was required of both blacks and whites, white voters usually got an easier exam. For example, while a white applicant might be asked to read aloud a single sentence from the Constitution, a black applicant would have to read a long, complicated paragraph. Tests given to blacks usually included convoluted sentences or confusingly worded questions. The administrator of the test, who was always white, evaluated the exams, and often only one wrong answer on a long test was enough for failure.

Poll taxes and literacy tests proved very effective in disenfranchising African Americans. It would take more than half a century and another constitutional amendment to finally end voting discrimination in America.

Organizing for Action

In April 1966, civil rights activist Ella Baker founded the Student Nonviolent Coordinating Committee (SNCC, pronounced *snick*) at a conference of sit-in leaders at Shaw University in Raleigh, North Carolina. The group's guiding purpose was to provide a unified organization through which student protesters could coordinate nonviolent activism to advance the goals of the Civil Rights Movement. Baker persuaded Dr. Martin Luther King Jr. to donate $800 to fund the conference.

Among those in attendance at the conference were Marion Berry (who would later become the mayor of Washington, DC), and activists John Lewis, James Bevel, Bernard Lafayette, and Diane Nash, all of whom would become leaders in the Civil Rights Movement. SNCC became an important part of the movement with its participation in sit-ins, Freedom Rides, and the 1963

Ella Baker (left) founded the Student Nonviolent Coordinating Committee (SNCC). The group's guiding purpose was to provide a unified organization for students to coordinate nonviolent protests.

March on Washington for Jobs and Freedom. Soon the organization turned its efforts toward African American voter registration in the South.

Robert Moses was a mathematics teacher when he became involved in the Civil Rights Movement. Born in Harlem, a black neighborhood of New York City, and educated at Harvard University, Moses became a field representative for SNCC in 1960. His job was to travel to southern states to recruit volunteer civil rights workers for SNCC.

Fannie Lou Hamer: Crusader for Voting Rights

Born in 1917 in Montgomery County, Mississippi, to sharecropper parents, Fannie Lou Townsend grew up under the hardships of the South's Jim Crow laws. As a child, Fannie helped her family pick cotton. She also loved to read, but her schooling was often interrupted by the needs of farm work.

Fannie married Perry Hamer and settled in Sunflower County, Mississippi, where they continued sharecropping. In 1962, Fannie Hamer's interest in civil rights was sparked by her attendance at a local SNCC meeting. She became a field secretary for the organization and began working on voter registration campaigns. In Mississippi, this was dangerous work. In June 1963, Hamer and several others were arrested in Winona, Mississippi, after conducting a voter training session. Locked up in the local jail, Hamer and the others received vicious beatings by police.

Hamer was a founder of the Mississippi Freedom Democratic Party (MFDP) and in August 1964 was an MFDP delegate to the Democratic National Convention. Speaking before the convention's Credentials Committee, Hamer recounted her brutal jail experience in a heartfelt plea for her party's inclusion at the convention, but she could not convince the powerful Democrats to include the MFDP. Returning home to Mississippi, Hamer spent the rest of her life promoting civil rights and working to end poverty. She died in 1977, leaving a legacy of activism and compassion. Her tombstone bears one of her most famous sayings on racial injustice: "I am sick and tired of being sick and tired."

Quoted in "Fannie Lou Hamer: Civil Rights Activist, Activist, Philanthropist (1917–1977)." Biography. www.biography .com.

In the mid-twentieth century, Mississippi was the poorest state in the nation, especially for African Americans: 86 percent of black families in Mississippi lived below the federal poverty line. African Americans made up 45 percent of Mississippi's population, but only 5 percent of those eligible to vote were registered. A principal reason for this was a group called the Citizens' Council, which used intimidation and economic pressure to keep blacks from the polls. In 1962, Robert Moses and SNCC decided to make Mississippi the focus of their voting rights campaign.

The Freedom Vote

In 1963, under an umbrella organization called the Council of Federated Organizations (COFO), SNCC began plans for a mock election called the Freedom Vote to coincide with Mississippi's November election for governor. White southerners generally felt that blacks were not smart enough or interested enough to vote, and the Freedom Vote was a way to counteract that idea in Mississippi and set an example for the rest of the nation.

SNCC workers, mostly young, white college-age men and women, began educating black Mississippians on how to register to vote. Volunteers set up voter registration sites in local churches, barber shops, grocery stores, and pool halls across Mississippi. The Freedom Vote was held over a three-day period preceding the regular election on November 5. The turnout was impressive. An estimated total of some eighty thousand votes were recorded, despite harassment from white citizens and police who tried to discourage the black voters. At a postelection rally, Moses said, "These election returns . . . demonstrate the desire of the Negroes of Mississippi to vote. We already knew that; now all America must know it."[45]

> "These election returns . . . demonstrate the desire of the Negroes of Mississippi to vote. We already knew that; now all America must know it."[45]
>
> —Activist Robert Moses

1964: Freedom Summer

The success of the Freedom Vote paved the way for another, even more ambitious voting rights project. For two weeks in June 1964, some one thousand college-age volunteers descended on the campus of Western College for Women in Oxford, Ohio, to attend training sessions for the new initiative, the Mississippi Summer Project, also known as Freedom Summer.

Coordinated by COFO but run mostly by SNCC, Freedom Summer's goals were to register as many black voters as possible, create alternative Freedom Schools for black children, and establish community centers to provide legal and health services. A new political party, the Mississippi Freedom Democratic Party (MFDP), was established to challenge the state's all-white regular Democratic Party for the right to be represented at the Democratic National Convention in August 1964.

For the volunteers, who were mostly white, middle class, and well-educated, going to the epicenter of southern racial discrimination would be a new and unsettling experience. James Forman, executive secretary of SNCC, pulled no punches in describing the danger the volunteers would be facing. "I may be killed. You may be killed. The whole staff may go."[46] Such harsh reality was underscored by the preparations of Mississippi law enforcement. In Jackson, city officials recruited additional police and stockpiled shotguns and gas masks. An armored vehicle, named Thompson's Tank after Jackson's mayor, Allen C. Thompson, was readied in the event, however unlikely, that the volunteers would become violent.

Martin Luther King Jr. talks with a family at their home in Greenwood, Mississippi. He went door to door garnering voter support for a new political party called the Mississippi Freedom Democratic Party.

Violence did occur, but volunteers were the victims, not the instigators. As SNCC workers began arriving in Mississippi on June 21, three volunteers, Michael Schwerner, James Chaney, and Andrew Goodman, went missing while driving in Neshoba County, Mississippi. Two days later, FBI and other police investigators found their burned-out station wagon, a sign of foul play. On August 4, their bodies were discovered buried under an earthen dam. The three had all been shot; Chaney, the only black one, had also been severely beaten. Their killers were members of the Ku Klux Klan, including the local deputy sheriff.

The SNCC volunteers in Mississippi were shocked by the murders, but were not intimidated and continued working through the long, hot summer. The voting registration drive registered to vote seventeen hundred African Americans throughout Mississippi—not enough to call the project a clear success, but it was a beginning. Those who braved the hostility of the Mississippi segregationists to go to the courthouse to register provided an example for other African Americans to follow, leading them to enter polling places in other southern states.

Protesting in Alabama

When King visited Mississippi after Chaney, Goodman, and Schwerner had disappeared, he told a crowd at a rally, "We've got to shed ourselves of fear, and we've got to say to those who oppose us with violence that you can't stop us."[47] The next year, that violence would burst forth as protesters brought their quest for voting rights to Alabama.

In January 1965, King was president of the civil rights organization the Southern Christian Leadership Conference (SCLC), which was a major force in the Civil Rights Movement. He announced that the organization would stage protest marches against voting rights violations in Selma, Alabama. In Selma, literacy tests kept the number of registered African American voters to a scant 130 out of 15,000 who were eligible. Civil rights groups had met with staunch resistance when trying to register black citizens in Selma to vote. On February 1, some seven hundred protesters, including King, were arrested and jailed. On February 18, during a peaceful protest march in Marion, a town near Selma, twenty-six-year-old activist Jimmie Lee Jackson was shot by an Alabama state trooper. Jackson died from his wounds on February 26, fueling outrage from the protesters at the brutality of the police. Two days later, the Reverend James Bevel, a minister who was King's colleague in the SCLC, told a congregation in Selma that they should march the 54 miles (89.9 km) to Montgomery, the capital of Alabama. "We must go to Montgomery and see the king," he urged, the word "king" referring in biblical terms to George Wallace, Alabama's governor. He further exclaimed: "Be prepared to walk to Montgomery! Be prepared to sleep on the highway!"[48]

> "We must go to Montgomery and see the king. Be prepared to walk to Montgomery! Be prepared to sleep on the highway!"[48]
>
> —The Reverend James Bevel

King agreed with Bevel's idea, and set the date for the march to Montgomery for Sunday, March 7. Later that evening, Bevel announced detailed plans for the march. Both men knew that taking action allowed Selma's African American community to channel its anger over Jackson's murder into something constructive. What they could not know was the violence that would greet them on their journey.

Bloody Sunday

On Sunday, March 7, 1965, around six hundred marchers left Selma's Brown Chapel African Methodist Episcopal Church, led by John Lewis from SNCC and Hosea Williams of the SCLC. Their first objective was to cross the Edmund Pettus Bridge that spanned the Alabama River. Waiting on the other side of the bridge was a blockade of state troopers and other law enforcement officers, under orders from Wallace to stop the march.

Tear gas fills the air as police violently break up a voting rights demonstration march in Selma, Alabama, in 1965. Many protesters were seriously hurt, and the day would come to be known as Bloody Sunday.

When the marchers reached the far end of the bridge, Major John Cloud, commander of the state troopers, announced through a bullhorn, "This is an unlawful assembly. You are to disperse. You are ordered to disperse. Go home or go to your church. This march will not continue."[49] The two lines, marchers and troopers, stood silently with a span of some 50 feet (15 m) between them. After about a minute, the line of troopers, now wearing gas masks and carrying nightsticks, began closing the gap. As the groups converged, the troopers violently forced the marchers back over the bridge, raining down blows with their nightsticks on the unarmed protesters. Fallen marchers who were trampled in the confusion received kicks and more hits from the troopers' nightsticks. Soon a cloud of tear gas billowed over the scene, blinding and choking the retreating marchers. SNCC worker Lafayette Surney described the carnage over the phone to the SNCC office in Atlanta:

> Police are beating people on the streets. Oh, man, they're just picking them up and putting them in ambulances. People are getting hurt pretty bad. Ambulances are going

by with their sirens going. People are running, crying, telling what's happening.[50]

Television cameramen at the scene risked their lives to record the unfolding bloodshed. That night the television networks interrupted their prime-time programming to broadcast film of the mayhem at the Edmund Pettus Bridge, on a day that would come to be known as Bloody Sunday. The nation witnessed the lengths that some people would go to in order to prevent blacks from voting.

The Marches Continue

The marchers, undeterred by the brutal violence, vowed to continue their protests. Although King had been unable to join the first march, he would not miss the next one. He rallied the protesters for another attempt on March 9. This time, the crowd of protesters swelled to some two thousand. Once again, the marchers were confronted by a wall of state troopers at the end of the Edmund Pettus Bridge. Instead of pressing ahead, however, King instead stopped and led the marchers in prayer. After praying, the protesters were astonished to see the line of troopers slowly part, creating a path through which they could move forward. Unsure of what to do, the crowd looked to their leader. After a moment, King ordered the group to turn around and march back to the Brown Chapel.

The marchers were stunned. They wondered whether the violence of Bloody Sunday had caused King to lose his nerve. Still, they obeyed their leader and retreated, unaware that King had a plan. He was waiting for federal judge Frank M. Johnson to issue a ruling that would allow the march to proceed without obstruction by Alabama law enforcement authorities. Until then, under a secret deal he had made with a representative of President Johnson, King vowed

> "Police are beating people on the streets. Oh, man, they're just picking them up and putting them in ambulances. People are getting hurt pretty bad. . . . People are running, crying, telling what's happening."[50]
>
> —SNCC worker Lafayette Surney

Martyrs for the Cause

The Civil Rights Monument in Montgomery, Alabama, is a black granite disk inscribed with the names of forty-one people who died during the struggle for civil rights. Here are the stories of two of those martyrs.

Vernon Dahmer was a well-to-do African American businessman in Hattiesburg, Mississippi. After the passage of the Voting Rights Act of 1965, Dahmer announced that he would pay the poll tax for anyone who could not afford it. When the KKK learned of Dahmer's offer, they made him, in Klan parlance, a Project 3 and Project 4 target: marked for arson and murder. On January 9, 1966, Dahmer's home was set afire as he and his family were attacked by armed KKK members. Dahmer returned gun fire, allowing his family to escape to safety, but he died two days later of burns and smoke inhalation.

Viola Liuzzo, a white housewife, activist, and NAACP member from Detroit was disturbed by the images of Bloody Sunday violence she saw on television. She drove to Alabama to help the marchers by using her car to transport volunteers between Selma and Montgomery. On March 25, 1965, Liuzzo was driving a black worker home when a car filled with four men pulled alongside hers. The men were KKK members and were outraged at a woman driving a black man. Liuzzo sped up to try to outrun the other car, but it caught up again. One of the men fired several shots into Liuzzo's car, killing her; her black passenger escaped injury.

to avoid another confrontation. Johnson was keenly aware that the right to vote was crucial to the advancement of civil rights. On March 17, the Voting Rights Act was introduced in Congress. That same day, as Congress began the long process of enacting the bill into law, the marchers in Selma received some welcome news. King announced that Judge Johnson had ruled that the march to Montgomery could take place without interference. The crowd cheered at the news and began preparing for the march to Montgomery.

From Selma to Montgomery

On Sunday, March 21, a crowd of nearly three thousand marchers set off on the first leg of the march to Montgomery. Led by King, John Lewis, Hosea Williams, civil rights activist Ralph

Abernathy, and clergy representing numerous congregations, the crowd moved briskly forward, protected by members of the Alabama National Guard under the control of the federal government. At a point where the highway narrowed from four lanes to two, the crowd had to be reduced to three hundred marchers by Judge Johnson's order. The rest were transported back to Selma, but most would later rejoin the march where the road once more widened.

In weather that was alternately rainy and sunny, with temperatures that fell to below freezing at night, the marchers walked along the highway, singing freedom songs to keep their spirits up. On March 25, the protesters at last reached their destination: the capitol building in Montgomery. By then the crowd had swelled to some twenty-five thousand. At a rally in front of the capitol, the crowd listened to speeches by Lewis, Bevel, King, and other civil rights leaders. A delegation of marchers attempted to deliver a petition to Wallace seeking the right to vote, but the governor refused to meet with them. It was reported that he watched the rally through the blinds in his office.

> "Wherever, by clear and objective standards, states and counties are using regulations, or laws, or tests to deny the right to vote, then they will be struck down."[51]
>
> —President Lyndon B. Johnson

On August 6, President Johnson signed the landmark Voting Rights Act of 1965 into law. Before signing the bill, Johnson said, "Wherever, by clear and objective standards, states and counties are using regulations, or laws, or tests to deny the right to vote, then they will be struck down."[51] From that day forward, no one could legally be denied the right to vote in the United States because of race or color. Lewis later remarked, "President Johnson signed that act, but it was written by the people of Selma."[52] It was written in the blood of the brave marchers who risked, and sometimes lost, their lives to gain voting equality for all African Americans.

CHAPTER FIVE

Civil Rights in the Twenty-First Century

The historic journey that led to the Civil Rights Act of 1964 focused on securing equality for African Americans in voting, education, housing, and employment. Since then, blacks have participated in choosing their elected officials, have succeeded in every profession, and have won numerous discrimination lawsuits. Over the last half century, African Americans have continued to fight to retain rights that are essential to America's national ideals. In 2014, Speaker of the House of Representatives Paul Ryan stated that the American way of life is "made possible by our commitment to the principles of freedom and equality—and rooted in our respect for every person's natural rights."[53] But some observers argue that these rights are still not fully respected in the twenty-first century.

De Facto Segregation

Denying opportunities to people of certain races or ethnicities by actions or business practices is called de facto segregation— discrimination practiced "in fact" even though prohibited by law. In the twenty-first century, critics claim that de facto segregation still exists, in the form of exclusive whites-only housing, limited employment opportunities for minorities, economic inequality, and separation in social and political situations.

A practice known as redlining was used by lenders beginning in the 1930s to deny mortgage loans to minorities seeking housing in mostly white neighborhoods. Redlining resulted in the growth of poor inner-city areas, the only places where minorities could afford to live. Although it is now illegal, redlining still occurs. A 2018 study found that in sixty-one municipalities, there is a higher denial rate of conventional mortgages for minorities looking to buy in predominantly white neighborhoods. In Detroit, for example, in 2016, black loan applicants were almost twice as likely to be rejected for a loan than were white applicants.

Another aspect of this type of discrimination is called retail redlining, in which businesses such as restaurants, grocery stores, and other retailers refuse to do business in certain communities due to their racial composition. In Olympia Fields, Illinois, an integrated Chicago suburb, village administrator David Mekarski was told that upscale restaurants were reluctant to build in his city because "black folks don't tip, and so managers can't maintain a quality staff. And if they can't maintain a quality staff, they can't maintain a quality restaurant." Shocked, Mekarski later commented, "This is one of the most pervasive and insidious forms of racism left in America today."[54]

A young couple applies for a home mortgage. Studies have shown that in many areas of the country black loan applicants are significantly more likely to be rejected for a loan than are white applicants.

Pervasive racism in the twenty-first century touches many areas of life, including economic status, employment, social mobility, and housing. But when it comes to the victims of racism, schoolchildren have the most to lose.

Resegregating Schools

The Civil War began with the secession of eleven southern states from the Union. In the twenty-first century, a new kind of secession is taking place. This form of secession involves school districts rather than states. The goal, critics argue, is to separate white students from black students.

In 2010, the town of Gardendale in Jefferson County, Alabama, had a population of nearly fourteen thousand, of whom 88.4 percent were white, and 8.6 percent were African American. In 2013, residents of Gardendale decided to secede from the Jefferson County School District and form a new district of their own. The proponents of the change did not explicitly cite race as a cause for their decision, stating that their already overcrowded schools were being burdened by students (implicitly meaning minority students) bused to Gardendale schools from other communities. According to a Facebook post by the Gardendale activists, they were only seeking "better control over the geographic composition of the student body."[55] The students being bused in, they said, were enjoying the advantages of Gardendale schools even though their parents were not supporting the district with taxes.

In April 2017, a federal district judge granted permission for Gardendale to form its own school district. The judge, Madeline Haikala, granted the request despite her finding that the secession was racially motivated, voicing her concern that the black students would ultimately be blamed, and perhaps bullied, for blocking Gardendale's effort to improve its school system. Plans were going forward when, in February 2018, an appeals court reversed Haikala's ruling, leaving both black and white parents pondering the uncertain future of their children's education.

Gardendale was not the first community in Jefferson County to seek its own school district: eight other communities had already seceded. And Alabama is not the only state to be affected by such school district changes. A 2014 study conducted by the University of California, Los Angeles, revealed "a vast transformation of the nation's school population since the civil rights era."[56] The study shows an initial growth in the percentage of black students attending majority white schools from 0 percent in 1954, the year *Brown* was decided, to a high of 43.5 percent in 1988. From that point, however, the numbers decline, falling to 23.2 percent in 2011. Another study conducted by the US government reports a doubling of schools primarily serving minorities. US Representative John Conyers of Michigan noted that such surveys confirm "what has long been feared and proves that current barriers against educational equality are eerily similar to those fought during the civil rights movement."[57]

> "Current barriers against educational equality are eerily similar to those fought during the civil rights movement."[57]
>
> —US Representative John Conyers

Undermining the Voting Rights Act

Along with education, advances in voting rights have come under attack. In 2013, the US Supreme Court was challenged to rule on the relevance of the Voting Rights Act of 1965 in the twenty-first century. *Shelby County v. Holder* centered around two sections of the Voting Rights Act. Section 5 requires certain states or local governments to obtain federal permission, or precertification, before changing or instituting any voting rules that may impact minorities' right to vote. Section 4 presents a formula for determining which states or local governments are subject to the provisions of Section 5. Most states that have a history of discriminatory voting practices fell under the formula. In the lawsuit, Shelby County, Alabama, sought to have these two sections declared unconstitutional. On June 25, 2013, the court ruled that Section 4 was indeed unconstitutional because its formula was obsolete, as voting conditions had changed since the Voting Rights Act was passed. The court did not find Section 5 unconstitutional, but without Section 4 to determine which states or local governments were subject to the precertification requirement, there was no way to enforce it.

Critics saw the result of *Shelby County v. Holder* as an elimination of a vital protection concerning the right to vote. Without the safeguards of Section 5, new and possibly discriminatory requirements for voting could be instituted without the consent of the federal government. "The Supreme Court has effectively gutted one of the nation's most important and effective civil rights laws," wrote civil rights attorney Jon Greenbaum. He added, "Minority voters in places with a record of discrimination are now at greater

African Americans in Office

One measure of civil rights progress can be found in the number of African American elected officials serving in local, state, and federal governments. In 1870, during the Reconstruction era, Hiram Rhodes Revels, a minister and chaplain for the Union Army in the Civil War, was the first black person elected to the United States Senate. A Republican, Revels represented his home state of Mississippi. Since then, some 153 African Americans have served in Congress.

When the 115th Congress convened in 2017, it was the most racially diverse in history. As of January 2018, there were a record number of African Americans in Congress: forty-eight in the House of Representatives and three in the Senate. Women and Hispanics also made gains in congressional representation.

The most historic example of the political progress of minorities in the twenty-first century was the election of Barack Obama as the nation's first African American president. After graduating from Harvard Law School, Obama became a civil rights lawyer and law professor. Before beginning his political career, he was a community organizer in Chicago with the faith-based Developing Communities Project, assisting low-income residents of some of the city's poorest South Side neighborhoods.

In 2014, *USA Today* reported that the number of African Americans at all levels of government rose from 1,469 in 1970 to 10,500 in 2014, a more than sevenfold increase. From a president to a city council member, black influence in government is on the rise.

risk of being disenfranchised than they have been in decades. Today's decision is a blow to democracy."[58]

Since the Supreme Court decision, many states have instituted new voting laws, some of which are opposed by civil rights activists. For example, laws requiring a voter to present a photo ID card to vote have been enacted in many jurisdictions. Having a driver's license qualifies as valid identification, but people who do not drive must obtain another form of ID. Most states issue photo IDs for nondrivers. However, critics worry that it may be difficult for the poor to get to an office that issues the cards or to assemble the proper proof-of-identity documents needed to get an ID. Without an ID, says lawyer Abbie Kamin, "many people will give up and not even bother trying to vote."[59] There is also political fallout over voter IDs. A study conducted by the University of California, San Diego, from 2008 to 2012 concluded that because many poor minorities vote liberal, "by instituting strict photo ID laws, states could minimize the influence of voters on the left and could dramatically alter the political leaning of the electorate."[60]

The change in the Voting Rights Act means that the only way to challenge new voting laws that are seen as discriminatory is through the courts, a costly and time-consuming process. Even so, a law can only be challenged once it is already on the books, and while a case is in court, sometimes for years, many potential voters may lose their right to cast a ballot.

A Controversial Killing

While the right to vote is the foundation of American democracy, there is perhaps no more personal right than that of being able to live without fear of being harmed or killed. Many people, however, believe that that right has never been secured for African Americans. On the evening of February 26, 2012, Trayvon Martin left a convenience store in Sanford, Florida, carrying a bottle of iced tea and a bag of Skittles candy. Martin, a seventeen-year-old African American, was walking back to his father's fiancée's townhome in a gated community called the Retreat at Twin Lakes. At the same time, twenty-eight-year-old George Zimmerman, a resident and member of the community's neighborhood watch program, was patrolling the dark streets of the Retreat in his truck. Upon noticing Martin, Zimmerman called 911, telling the dispatcher, "We've had some break-ins in my neighborhood, and there's a real suspicious guy."[61] Despite being told to stay in his truck by the 911 dispatcher, Zimmerman got out and approached Martin. During the confrontation that ensued, Zimmerman fired one shot from a 9 mm pistol he carried, killing the teenager.

Outrage in the African American community over the killing of the unarmed youth was immediate. It further intensified on July 13, 2013, when Zimmerman was acquitted of second-degree murder

Protesters rally in support of Trayvon Martin, a seventeen-year-old African American boy who was shot and killed by George Zimmerman. Zimmerman was tried for murder and found not guilty.

after the Florida jury determined that he shot Martin in self-defense. In Oakland, California, African American activist Alicia Garza was following the progress of the Zimmerman jury on her phone. When the verdict came in, Garza was stunned. "As a black person," she later recalled, "I felt incredibly vulnerable, incredibly exposed and incredibly enraged. . . . It was a verdict that said: black people are not safe in America."[62] She vowed to do something about it.

Black Lives Matter

Garza immediately took to Facebook and posted, "I continue to be surprised at how little black lives matter. And I will continue that. Stop giving up on black life. Black people, I will NEVER give up on us. NEVER."[63] Patrisse Cullors, an activist and friend of Garza, replied to the post using the hashtag #BlackLivesMatter (BLM), and a movement was born. Garza and Cullors, along with Opal Tometi, another friend, began discussing how they could use social media to address the issues of racism and violence against African Americans. From its beginning with three women, BLM has grown, as of 2018, to include forty chapters across the United States, Canada, and Britain, linked not by proximity but by the social media hashtag #BlackLivesMatter.

Bringing the issue of police violence against blacks to mainstream America by using direct action is one of the main goals of BLM. Such action was evident in two high-profile cases: the 2014 deaths of Michael Brown in Ferguson, Missouri, and Eric Garner in New York City. Both cases involved the deaths of African American males by white police officers. During a riot that broke out in Ferguson after the Brown shooting, protesters filled the streets chanting "Black lives matter!" New York City and Los Angeles also saw protests by BLM activists. Since then, BLM

A woman supports the Black Lives Matter movement at a rally in Washington, DC. The movement began in 2013 from a few Facebook posts expressing frustration over violence against African Americans.

has protested the deaths of such victims as Sandra Bland, Tamir Rice, and Freddie Gray, all African Americans who died by a police officer's gunfire or while in police custody.

Not everyone agrees with the actions and motives of Black Lives Matter. For example, former Chicago police superintendent Garry McCarthy views BLM as "a movement with the goal of saving black lives [that] at this point is getting black lives taken, because 80 percent of our murder victims here in Chicago are male blacks."[64] Activist Brittany Packnett disagrees, saying that BLM "is an acknowledgement of the fact that black lives, brown lives, that people of color in particular, are the ones suffering disproportionately from issues of police brutality."[65] Despite differing opinions, the BLM's goals of using media and mass demonstrations to create awareness of racial discrimination are twenty-first-century echoes of the activism and ideals of the original Civil Rights Movement.

White Supremacy Rises

During Reconstruction, the Ku Klux Klan terrorized newly freed African Americans, burning crosses in front of their homes and staging public lynchings of innocent black men. In the twenty-first century, the KKK and other white supremacist groups have again taken to the streets to disseminate their racial hatred.

In August 2017, white supremacists descended on the college town of Charlottesville, Virginia, to protest the planned removal of a statue of Confederate general Robert E. Lee. The rally, called "Unite the Right," was described by the Southern Poverty Law Center (SPLC) as the largest supremacist rally of its kind in decades. During the rally one person was killed and some thirty others injured when a white supremacist drove his car into a crowd of counterprotesters there to confront the supremacists. Charlottesville mayor Michael Signer later said the gathering was "either profoundly ignorant or was designed to instill fear in our minority populations in a way that harkens back to the days of the KKK."

In 2017, the SPLC noted that there were some sixteen hundred extremist groups operating in the United States, including the KKK and the so-called alt-right movement. Made up of numerous hate groups, the alt-right believes in white nationalism (the concept of a majority-white America), an end to nonwhite immigration, and the general superiority of the white race over all others. As of 2018, alt-right groups have been responsible for more than one hundred deaths and injuries, and some suggest that they should be classified as terrorists.

Quoted in Madison Park, "Why White Nationalists Are Drawn to Charlottesville," CNN, August 12, 2017. www .cnn.com.

Black Economics: Progress and Retreat

At the end of World War II, most African Americans were trapped in a life of poverty, earning little as manual laborers, farmhands, and domestic workers. Only about 5 percent of black men held white-collar jobs that paid more than a minimal wage. Throughout the 1960s and 1970s that situation began to change as African Americans benefited from increased opportunities in education, changing attitudes in employment, and the advances brought about by civil rights legislation. By the late 1990s, it seemed that African Americans were making steady progress in terms of jobs and income. Many believe, however, that progress has stalled in the twenty-first century.

A report issued by the Economic Policy Institute in 2018 traced the economic progress that African Americans had made over the previous fifty years. According to the report, blacks had made significant strides in education, with over 90 percent obtaining high school diplomas, as well as being more than twice as likely to have graduated from college compared to 1968. But these advances have not translated to economic improvement, the report found. It noted: "Black workers still make only 82.5 cents on every dollar earned by white workers, African Americans are 2.5 times as likely to be in poverty as whites, and the median white family has almost 10 times as much wealth as the median black family."[66] In 2017, the black unemployment rate of 7.5 percent remained higher than that of whites, at 3.8 percent. At the top of the corporate ladder in 2018 there were only three African American CEOs in the five hundred largest US corporations, a number that fell from six CEOs in 2012.

A Jim Crow Economy

Birmingham, Alabama, the scene of so many civil rights protests in the 1960s, entered a new fight in the twenty-first century. In 2015, the Birmingham City Council voted to raise the city's minimum wage to $10.10 an hour, a higher wage than the federally mandated $7.25 an hour. In response, state lawmakers immediately passed legislation overturning the city council's vote. The legislators who opposed the increase were all white; the city council had a majority of black members. Scott Douglas, executive director of Greater Birmingham Ministries, said of the legislators, "They treated Birmingham like it had whistled at a white woman. It was like an insult: 'How dare you raise your own minimum wage without our say-so.'"[67] In a city where 74 percent of the population is African American, and

> "They treated Birmingham like it had whistled at a white woman. It was like an insult: 'How dare you raise your own minimum wage without our say-so.'"[67]
>
> —Scott Douglas, Greater Birmingham Ministries

32 percent of African Americans live below the poverty line, the wage increase would be most beneficial to the poorest citizens of Birmingham.

"The days of a Jim Crow economy should be long gone,"[68] comments Christine Owens, director of a nonprofit group promoting wage fairness. But the battle remains, and has spread nationally. While some twenty-one states and forty-one municipalities have raised their minimum wage above the federal level, twenty-four states have passed legislation negating such increases. In Birmingham, the first southern city to attempt to raise its minimum wage, the fight against Jim Crow attitudes continues.

A Significant Legacy for All Americans

The United States is home to a diverse population, including people of different backgrounds, colors, faiths, and ethnicities. But for all these differences, there is a common thread: that each person is entitled to basic civil rights that grant him or her freedom, safety, and dignity. Without the Civil Rights Movement, many of these rights would still be denied to people who differ from the majority in their identities, beliefs, or ways of life. With sit-ins, protest marches, calls for legislation, and the blood of martyrs, those fighting for civil rights have brought the nation closer to the ideals of the Founders and the principles of "life, liberty, and the pursuit of happiness."

SOURCE NOTES

Introduction: Equal Rights for All

1. Quoted in Katharine Greider, "The Schoolteacher on the Streetcar," *New York Times*, November 13, 2005. www.ny times.com.
2. Declaration of Independence. National Archives. www.ar chives.gov.

Chapter One: From Slavery to Jim Crow

3. Quoted in Henry Louis Gates, Jr., "The African Americans: Many Rivers to Cross: What Is Juneteenth?" PBS. www.pbs .org.
4. "Transcript of 13th Amendment to the U.S. Constitution: Abolition of Slavery (1865)." *Our Documents*. www.ourdocu ments.gov.
5. Quoted in Eric Foner, *Reconstruction: America's Unfinished Revolution, 1863–1877.* New York: Harper & Row, 1988, p. 199.
6. Quoted in Abigail Perkiss, "Federalism in 1868 and 2012." *Constitution Daily* (blog), April 9, 2012. www.constitution center.org.
7. Quoted in Foner, *Reconstruction*, p. 425.
8. Quoted in Foner, *Reconstruction*, p. 438.
9. "Transcript of 14th Amendment to the U.S. Constitution: Civil Rights (1868)." Our Documents. www.ourdocuments.gov.
10. "Transcript of 15th Amendment to the U.S. Constitution: Voting Rights (1870)." Our Documents. www.ourdocuments.gov.
11. Quoted in Foner, *Reconstruction*, p. 448.
12. Quoted in Edward L. Ayers, Lewis L. Gould, David M. Oshinsky, Jean R. Soderlund, *American Passages: A History of the United States,* vol. 2, *Since 1865*. Boston: Wadsworth, 2012, p. 347.
13. W.E.B. Dubois, "Niagara Movement Speech." www.teaching americanhistory.org.
14. "Transcript of Executive Order 9981: Desegregation of the Armed Forces (1948)." Our Documents. www.ourdocuments .gov.

Chapter Two: Demonstrating for Equality

15. Quoted in Fred Powledge, *Free at Last? The Civil Rights Movement and the People Who Made It.* New York: Little, Brown, 1991, p. 199.
16. Quoted in Andrew Cohen, "The Black Students Who Wouldn't Leave the Lunch Counter," *Atlantic*, January 10, 2014. www.theatlantic.com.
17. Quoted in "American Radio Works: Segregation in Public Places: Jim Crow Was Painful," American Public Media. www.apmreports.org.
18. David Halberstam, *The Fifties*. New York: Random House, 1993, p. 437.
19. *Commonweal*, September 23, 1955. Quoted in Sanford Wexler, *The Civil Rights Movement: An Eyewitness History*. New York: Facts On File, 1993, pp. 64–65.
20. Quoted in Lynne Olson, *Freedom's Daughters: The Unsung Heroines of the Civil Rights Movement from 1830 to 1970*. New York: Scribner, 2001, p. 108.
21. Quoted in Ann Bausum, *Freedom Riders: John Lewis and Jim Zwerg on the Front Lines of the Civil Rights Movement*. Washington, DC: National Geographic, 2006, p. 44.
22. Quoted in Sanford Wexler, *The Civil Rights Movement: An Eyewitness History*. New York: Facts On File, 1993, p. 118.
23. FR Project: Jim Zwerg in Hospital. YouTube. www.youtube.com.
24. Quoted in Jack Doyle, "Buses Are A'Comin'—Freedom Riders: 1961," Pop History Dig, June 24, 2014. PopHistoryDig.com.
25. Quoted in Tim Molloy, "How MLK Ad-Libbed the 'I Have a Dream' Speech," *Wrap*, January 15, 2018. www.thewrap.com.
26. Martin Luther King Jr., "'I Have a Dream,' Address Delivered at the March on Washington for Jobs and Freedom," August 28, 1963, Stanford University, The Martin Luther King, Jr. Research and Education Institute. https://kinginstitute.stanford.edu.
27. Quoted in William P. Jones, *The March on Washington: Jobs, Freedom, and the Forgotten History of Civil Rights*. New York: Norton, 2013, p. 200.

Chapter Three: Ending School Segregation

28. Quoted in "Eyewitness to Jim Crow: Joan Johns Cobb Remembers," The History of Jim Crow. www.jimcrowhistory.org.
29. Quoted in "Linda Brown: Activist, Civil Rights Activist," Biography. www.biography.com.
30. Quoted in Leon Friedman, ed., *Brown v. Board: The Landmark Oral Argument Before the Supreme Court*. New York: New Press, 1969, p. 38.
31. Quoted in Friedman, ed., *Brown v. Board*, p. 67.
32. Quoted in Friedman, ed., *Brown v. Board*, pp. 329–30.
33. Quoted in Juan Williams, *Thurgood Marshall: American Revolutionary*. New York: Times Books, 1998, p. 229.
34. Quoted in Wexler, *The Civil Rights Movement*, pp. 48–49.
35. Quoted in George Barrett, "Bus Integration in Alabama Calm," *New York Times*, December 22, 1956. Quoted in Wexler, *The Civil Rights Movement*, p. 85.
36. Quoted in "Little Rock Central High School," Little Rock Central High School/Hall High School. www.lrchs-hall.com.
37. Carlotta Walls LaNier, *A Mighty Long Way: My Journey to Justice at Little Rock Central High School*. New York: One World, 2009, p. 45.
38. LaNier, *A Mighty Long Way*, p. 53.
39. Quoted in Roy Reed, *Faubus: The Life and Times of an American Prodigal*. Fayetteville: University of Arkansas, 1997, p. 178.
40. Quoted in Wexler, *The Civil Rights Movement*, p. 89.
41. Quoted in Juan Williams, *Eyes on the Prize: America's Civil Rights Years, 1954–1965*. New York: Penguin, 1988, p. 113.
42. Quoted in *Time*, "The Meaning of Little Rock," October 7, 1957. www.time.com.

Chapter Four: Securing the Right to Vote

43. Quoted in "Thomas Peterson Casts the First Vote," The History Engine. www.historyengine.richmond.edu.
44. "Transcript of 15th Amendment to the U.S. Constitution: Voting Rights (1870)." Our Documents. www.ourdocuments.gov.
45. Quoted in Joseph A. Sinsheimer, "The Freedom Vote of 1963: New Strategies of Racial Protest in Mississippi." *Journal of Southern History*, May 1989, pp. 241–42.

46. Quoted in Williams, *Eyes on the Prize*, p. 230.
47. Quoted in Taylor Branch, *Pillar of Fire: America in the King Years, 1963–65*. New York: Simon & Schuster, 1998, p. 414.
48. Quoted in Taylor Branch, *At Canaan's Edge: America in the King Years, 1965–68*. New York: Simon & Schuster, 2006, p. 9.
49. Quoted in Branch, *At Canaan's Edge*, p. 50.
50. Quoted in Branch, *At Canaan's Edge*, p. 51.
51. Lyndon B. Johnson, "Remarks in the Capitol Rotunda at the Signing of the Voting Rights Act, August 6, 1965," The American Presidency Project. www.presidency.ucsb.edu.
52. Quoted in Annie Nelson, "Selma Brought Us a Voting Bill," Denver Public Library, Genealogy, African American and Western History Resources, February 10, 2015. https://history.denverlibrary.org.

Chapter Five: Civil Rights in the Twenty-First Century

53. Paul Ryan, *The Way Forward: Renewing the American Idea*. New York: Twelve, 2014, p. x.
54. Quoted in Emily Badger, "Retail Redlining: One of the Most Pervasive Forms of Racism Left in America?" Citylab, April 17, 2013. www.citylab.com.
55. Quoted in Nikole Hannah-Jones, "The Resegregation of Jefferson County," *New York Times Magazine*, September 6, 2107. www.nytimes.com.
56. Gary Orfield and Erica Frankenberg, with Jongyeon Ee and John Kuscera, "Brown at 60: Great Progress, a Long Retreat, and an Uncertain Future," The Civil Rights Project, University of California, Los Angeles, May 15, 2014. www.civilrightsproject.ucla.edu.
57. Quoted in Greg Toppo, "GAO Study: Segregation Worsening in U.S. Schools," *USA Today*, May 17, 2016. www.usatoday.com.
58. Quoted in Ryan J. Reilly, Mike Sacks, and Sabrina Siddiqui, "Voting Rights Act Section 4 Struck Down by Supreme Court," *Huffington Post*, June 25, 2013. www.huffingtonpost.com.

59. Quoted in Sari Horwitz, "Getting a Photo ID So You Can Vote Is Easy. Unless You're Poor, Black, Latino or Elderly," *Washington Post*, May 23, 2016. www.washingtonpost.com.
60. Quoted in Horwitz, "Getting a Photo ID So You Can Vote Is Easy."
61. Quoted in Chris Francescani, "George Zimmerman: Prelude to a Shooting," Reuters, April 25, 2012. www.reuters.com.
62. Quoted in Elizabeth Day, "#BlackLivesMatter: The Birth of a New Civil Rights Movement," *Guardian* (Manchester, UK), July 19, 2015. www.theguardian.com.
63. Quoted in Patrisse Khan-Cullors and Asha Bandede, *When They Call You a Terrorist: A Black Lives Matter Memoir*. New York: St. Martin's, 2017, p.180.
64. Quoted in Chris Sommerfeldt, "Ex-Chicago Top Cop Blames Black Lives Matter for Surge in Murders," *New York Daily News*, January 3, 2017. www.nydailynews.com.
65. Quoted in Day, "#BlackLivesMatter."
66. Quoted in Janelle Jones, John Schmitt, and Valerie Wilson, "50 Years After the Kerner Commission: African Americans Are Better Off in Many Ways But Are Still Disadvantaged by Racial Inequality," Ecomonic Policy Institute, February 26, 2018. www.epi.org.
67. Quoted in John Blake, "The Fight for $15 Takes On the 'Jim Crow Economy'," CNN, April 13, 2018. www.cnn.com.
68. Quoted in Blake, "The Fight for $15 Takes On the 'Jim Crow Economy'."

FOR FURTHER RESEARCH

Books

Carson Clayborne, *Civil Rights Chronicle: The African-American Struggle for Freedom*. Lincolnwood, IL: Legacy, 2003.

Karlyn Forner, *Why the Vote Wasn't Enough for Selma*. Durham, NC: Duke University Press, 2017.

Christopher J. Lebron, *The Making of Black Lives Matter: A Brief History of an Idea*. New York: Oxford University Press, 2017.

Steven Levingston, *Kennedy and King: The President, the Pastor, and the Battle over Civil Rights*. New York: Hachette, 2017.

John Lewis, Andrew Aydin, and Nate Powell, *March,* Books 1–3. Marietta, GA: Top Shelf Productions, 2013, 2015, 2016.

Susan Goldman Rubin, Brown v. Board of Education: *A Fight for Simple Justice*. New York: Holiday House, 2016.

Michael Shally-Jensen, *Defining Documents in American History: Civil Rights (1954–2015)*. Amenia, NY: Grey House, 2015.

Internet Sources

Joan Johns Cobb, "Eyewitness to Jim Crow: Joan Johns Cobb Remembers," http://www.core-online.org/History/barbara_johns 1.htm.

Andrew Cohen, "The Black Students Who Wouldn't Leave the Lunch Counter," *Atlantic*, January 10, 2014. www.theatlantic .com/national/archive/2014/01/the-black-students-who-wouldnt -leave-the-lunch-counter/282986.

Jack Doyle, "Buses Are A'Comin'—Freedom Riders: 1961," The Pop History Dig. www.pophistorydig.com/topics/freedom-riders -1961.

Garrett Epps, "Happy 14th Amendment Day!," *Salon*, July 21, 2006. www.salon.com/2006/07/21/14th_amendment.

Sam Fulwood III, "A Voting Rights Story: Injustice in North Carolina," Center for American Progress, July 22, 2016. www.american progress.org/issues/race/reports/2016/07/22/141713/a-voting -rights-story.

Nikole Hannah-Jones, "The Resegregation of Jefferson County," *New York Times Magazine*, September 6, 2017. www.nytimes .com/2017/09/06/magazine/the-resegregation-of-jefferson -county.html.

Lina Mai, "'I Had a Right to Be at Central': Remembering Little Rock's Integration Battle," *Time*, September 22, 2017. http:// time.com/4948704/little-rock-nine-anniversary.

Ashitha Nagesh, "Could You Pass This Test Given to Black People Registering to Vote in America in 1964?," *Metro*, September 20, 2017. http://metro.co.uk/2017/09/20/could-you-pass-this-test -given-to-black-people-registering-to-vote-in-america-in-1964 -6941338.

Adam Weinstein and the MoJo News Team, "The Trayvon Martin Killing, Explained," *Mother Jones*, March 18, 2012. www.mother jones.com/politics/2012/03/what-happened-trayvon-martin -explained.

Websites

Black Lives Matter (www.blacklivesmatter.com). This is the official website of the Black Lives Matter movement. In contains a history of the movement, resources for BLM action, and profiles of the movement's founders and regional organizers.

Civil Rights Digital Library (http://crdl.usg.edu). One of the most comprehensive efforts to deliver educational content on the Civil Rights Movement via the web, this site features links to civil rights information from educational organizations, libraries, government agencies, and other sources across the United States.

Civil Rights Movement Veterans (www.crmvet.org). This website was created by people who were involved firsthand in the Civil Rights Movement. It includes numerous resources such as photos, documents, articles, a timeline, and poetry about the movement.

Explore: Civil Rights Movement (1954–1985) (www.pbs.org /black-culture/explore/civil-rights-movement). This site explores all aspects of the Civil Rights Movement, from Freedom Rides to the Black Power Movement, with photos, videos, and quizzes.

Jim Crow Museum (https://ferris.edu/jimcrow). This website from Ferris State University in Michigan highlights artifacts from the Jim Crow years and includes a tour of the museum that can be viewed in standard or virtual reality modes.

Separate Is Not Equal: *Brown v. Board of Education* (http:// americanhistory.si.edu/brown/history). This site provides a comprehensive history of one of the most important cases heard by the US Supreme Court.

The King Encyclopedia (https://kinginstitute.stanford.edu/en cyclopedia). Dedicated to civil rights leader Martin Luther King Jr., this site contains an exhaustive encyclopedia, a chronology of King's life, selected quotes, and audio of King's most famous speeches and sermons.

INDEX

78

PICTURE CREDITS